M000085635

Without Boundaries:

consent-based, non-coercive parenting and autonomous education

by Jan Fortune-Wood

"... I'm going to show ... a world without rules or controls, without borders or boundaries, a world where anything is possible. Where we go from there is a choice I leave to you."
(*The Matrix*, closing scene, spoken by the character, Neo.)

Educational Heretics Press

Published 2000 by Educational Heretics Press
113 Arundel Drive, Bramcote Hills, Nottingham NG9 3FQ

British Cataloguing in Publication Data

Fortune-Wood, Jan
> Without Boundaries: consent-based, non-coercive
> parenting and autonomous education
> 1.Parenting 2.Education 3.Autonomy in children
> 4.Education – Philosophy 5.Education – Aims and
> Objectives
> I.Title
> 370.1

ISBN   1-900219-17-4

Design and production: Educational Heretics Press

Cover design by John Haxby, Edinburgh EH6 6QH

Printed by Masterprint Plus Ltd. (Tel. 0115 939 1772)

Acknowledgements

Thanks are due to many people who helped with this book, whether directly or through inspiration. Thank you to Roland Meighan, who has remained supportive throughout this project. Thanks to Martine Archer and Sue Cvach, who proof-read the text for me with meticulous care. Thank you to Peter Tuffnell and Sue Cvach, who read my drafts and made valuable comments and suggestions.

Two special thanks remain. The first is to the *Taking Children Seriously* (TCS) community, those people who write on the Internet list and in the journal, and who have helped me make the journey this far in taking children seriously. It has been an enormous and life changing journey and I have needed, been given, and continue to be given, an enormous amount of support on the way. Thank you to all who have been involved and who go on supporting this radical and wonderful alternative. Most especially thanks to Sarah Lawrence for her support, clear thinking, humour and persistence.

Secondly, an enormous thanks to my family, my husband Mike and our four children. Finding and implementing *Taking Children Seriously* in our lives has been a difficult and richly rewarding experience. Together, we know that we have a very long way to go still and we are very aware of how fallible we are and how often we get things wrong. Despite our short-comings we are optimistic. We know that neither guilt nor defeatism are useful alternatives. Thanks are due to them for making this journey with me.

Jan Fortune-Wood
July 2000

Contents

Introduction

Doing it their way, (EHP April 2000) considers the primacy of intrinsic motivation in autonomous learning and contends that unimpeded growth of knowledge requires both a vastly increased definition of education and an abandoning of coercive parenting practices. *Without Boundaries,* substantively expands on this latter theme, arguing that both in theory and in practice, coercion is not only destructive of personal autonomy, but also inimical to learning and the growth of knowledge.

The theory of education and parenting developed in this book draws widely on the *Taking Children Seriously* (TCS) philosophy, an educational theory that has its roots in rationalism and in particular in the work of Karl Popper.

The book falls into two sections, with a concluding chapter drawing the themes together. The first part sets out a theory of non-coercion as it relates to parenting and education. It defines the terminology, examines the role of parents, and explores autonomy as the basis for true growth of knowledge.

The second section looks at how the theory relates to autonomous learning and parenting practice. It takes an in-depth look at the issues that arise in any transition to an autonomous process and is focussed on the idea that with non-coercive techniques all participants can be 'winners', using illustrative scenarios to demonstrate the point. In the central chapter of the book, the notion of boundaries as a central pillar of parenting and learning is deconstructed and a number of major issues in family life and learning are considered from a non-coercive perspective in order to demonstrate an alternative model of the growth of knowledge. This section also considers some of the more extreme fears that surround the process of de-coercing.

The final chapter sums up the preceding chapters and looks at the inclusiveness of this educational philosophy. It considers ways in which it might be applied across age ranges, individual personality differences, amongst families where members have been labeled with learning difficulties or syndromes or live with disabilities, and in situations where formal, structured education, including schooling, is viewed as an option by young people.

The *Taking Children Seriously* (TCS) philosophy, which is the inspiration of this book, is a wide-ranging and far-reaching theory that cannot be fully encompassed within the confines of one short book. I hope, however, to offer a broad introduction to a way of thinking that could revolutionise how we act as parents and how we think about education. In a world where parenting manuals proliferate, *Without Boundaries* offers a distinctively radical and practical alternative; not only a new paradigm for parenting, but one which deals with how, in a fast changing world, parenting and education must be integrated.

PART 1 introduction: A theory of non-coercion

Today's political climate is not largely one of educational experiment and diversity. The National Curriculum has become firmly lodged in people's minds as the blueprint of a proper education. The introduction of literacy, and now numeracy hours in schools have gone a long way to standardising educational experience for the vast majority of children. In a political climate of paternalism and rigorous standardisation, home educating parents stand out as what Roland Meighan has called a beacon of 'trail blazing'. Amongst those who exercise their legal right not to delegate the parental responsibility for education to either the state or private institutions, autonomous educators are a small but growing sub-set of people. Autonomous educators believe radically different things about learning and education. This book sets out to make their case and to do so particularly within the context of the British educational experience.

Whilst the thinkers who influence autonomously educating parents and children are, of course, international, there is a growing movement of people within the British Isles who question the logic of curricula, enforced teaching, adult-led subjects of learning and much more that goes with the mainstream package. Many of these parents have contributed to the later chapters of this book through sharing experiences of their own autonomous practice. Many others are attracted to the idea of autonomous, child-motivated education, but fear that it would result in a kind of stultifying nothingness or that it would take them beyond the boundaries of what is legally acceptable as an education. This book sets out to eradicate both of these myths and to make clearer the theory and practice which informs autonomous education.

Educational theory is not a homogenous or readily agreed upon body of knowledge. Over the course of the next three chapters, I aim to demonstrate that autonomous education is grounded in sound theory. This theoretical underpinning ensures that it is a valid and supportable lifestyle, which can be practised with confidence. I will begin with a brief overview of the thinking of those who have significantly influenced the trend to autonomous education, before moving on, in chapter two, to an examination of prevalent educational theories as they relate to autonomy. I will conclude part one of this book with a third chapter examining three broad schools of thinking within autonomous education; the theories of the natural child, 'unschooling' and non-coercion.

Chapter one

An alternative paradigm

Eradicating coercion is fundamental to real education. This is the premise of this book. It is not a common educational proposition, but it is one that I previously argued to be supportable both in educational theory and practice. (See *Doing It Their Way,* EHP 2000.) It is a premise that is gaining ground as more and more families not only choose home education, but also realise that the logical and moral extension of unschooling is to be found in the philosophy of the *Taking Children Seriously* (TCS) movement.

Coercion damages thinking

TCS philosophy maintains that coercion is detrimental to rational thinking and therefore damaging to education. This is an argument that I will explore more fully in Chapter 3, but, for many, it is an unfamiliar idea, which needs some introduction. Education and the optimum thought processes needed to learn are not simply, or even primarily, about being able to memorise and reproduce a received body of knowledge. They are essentially about the ability to create new knowledge and the best conditions for creativity and intrinsically motivated learning.

We are born with brains that are ideally suited to learning. We are born rational and creative. With the input of information and the unimpeded ability to learn through a continual process of conjecture and refutation, rational thought and creativity will develop and flourish. When the process is interrupted by coercion, however, a line of thought is sabotaged in its tracks. This sabotaging may often be accompanied by painful feelings of being thwarted and left in a state of turmoil. When this sabotaging occurs over and over again, especially in the same area, then in place of rational thinking there will be damaged thinking. A particular line of learning becomes cut off, while instead there is likely to be irrationality, poor theories, and a decrease in problem-solving capacity.

Let us imagine Jane, a five-year-old who has been brought up in a

family that tries hard to be child-centred. She has never been made
to sleep alone. At the age of four, she started to leave the family
bed of her own accord and now happily sleeps in her own bed. She
has never had a set bedtime, usually falling asleep by about 9.30 in
the evening, though sometimes later. Now she is going to school,
and her parents feel that it would be in her best interest for her to
have an evening routine including a set bedtime to ensure that she is
not too tired to get up for school each morning. Jane resists. For
several weeks there is conflict and tears. Fraught evenings and
disturbed nights replace the former harmony, but the parents persist,
convinced that they are doing the best thing. Eventually Jane gives
in. She forgets how to live by her own body clock and intrinsic
requirements. She grows up with poor theories about how much
sleep is needed regardless of personality and individual
requirements. She may well develop sleep problems at some stage
and wonder why.

Jane will be an incredibly lucky child if the coercion damage stops
there. In a family where well-meaning but coercive parents are
convinced that they know what is best, Jane is likely to have lots of
areas of her thinking damaged. She is sent to school and taught that
there is a list of essential things that she has to learn by a certain
age, even in a certain order, regardless of her own learning interests.
She may be withdrawn from school and home-educated, but still
subjected to what Roland Meighan has called the 'mythology' of
essential learning - those things that her parents deem 'necessary' for
her to know at a given time. It is likely that Jane's parents will want
to keep her safe, but in their anxiety they will replace the possibility
of Jane developing good, intrinsically motivated theories about the
best ways to stay safe, with extrinsic and artificial rules. Jane's
parents might be equally concerned about nutrition and thwart her
own explorations of food with theories about good and bad foods
until Jane is as confused as they are and develops eating disorders.

So how is Jane being damaged? The analogy of the growth of a
tree is one way to think about the growth of knowledge. Each act of
coercion opens a wound in a branch. Constant coercion in the same
area could remove a branch entirely. Something else may grow in
its place, but it will not be the same as the branch that would have
grown without impediment. Sometimes, completely alien branches
will be grafted on and they may grow well, but they are not what
the tree would have grown for itself. Coercion works. It is as
possible to produce moulded humans who fulfil certain behaviourist
outcomes as it is to grow cultivated, pruned trees or grafted trees or

stunted bonsai trees. The major difference is that it is not moral to rob another human of his or her autonomy in order to produce the specimen that a parent most desires, even when the desire is apparently fuelled by misguided notions of the child's own good. The analogy is limited, but it serves as an illustration of the damage that is caused to thinking by coercion.

Once the premise is accepted that coercion causes damaged thinking, education and life can never be the same again. This is not to say that parents have no role or that children should simply be left to their own devices. Rather, it demands a different model for problem solving and learning: a consensual, rational model in which everyone's ideas are equally valued, everyone's human fallibility is equally recognised, and everyone's autonomy is equally respected.

Then, how do we make the transition to non-coercive education and parenting? How is it possible to live family life without compromise? How can we always have win-win situations? How can responsible parents let go of the notion of boundaries?

The language of *Taking Children Seriously*

The language of this philosophy of non-coercive parenting and education, like the ideas it contains, is not always obvious. The key terminology gives us the tools for understanding this far-reaching paradigm. There is often a resistance to what is sometimes pejoratively called 'jargon' in parenting theories. TCS does use words in highly specific ways and sometimes in ways that make people feel uncomfortable. The theory is always open to improvement and to better ways of expressing its concepts. The definitions that have evolved, whilst they are distinctive and challenging, provide an accessible framework for unlocking what is a radically different approach to parenting.

Coercion

What do we mean by coercion? The shorthand TCS definition is 'anything that causes a person to enact one theory whilst another theory is still current in their mind'. A child washing up whilst she really wants to read a book, or a child who is made to put on smart clothes for a family dinner when he wants to go in his Buzz Light-year suit, would be very obvious examples. Likewise, a child who is doing a page of maths problems when she really wants to play computer games, provides another example.

But coercion is not always so blatant or obvious. Perhaps the child doing the page of maths problems has been told by her parents to clean her room. The child has just bought a brand new computer game that looks really fun and wants to be playing it. The parent, however, is insistent that the child should clean her room. The child responds that she was planning to do some maths (being aware that if she mentions the computer game the admonitions to clean the room will get much stronger). The parent approves of maths and agrees that this is a more worthwhile activity, at least for the time being. In the parent's hierarchy of activities, cleaning should not interrupt maths any more than playing computer games should interrupt cleaning. The child is left enacting one theory (doing maths), whilst another theory (playing the computer game), is active in her mind. She is in a state of coercion, even though she suggested doing the maths. If this kind of pattern persists, she is likely to develop thinking difficulties about maths and cleaning and computer games. How can she think rationally about these things when her mind is so full of coercion and tangled subterfuge?

Coercion can be very direct, but it can be equally subtle and manipulative. A child might be told that he is 'allowed' to watch television, but parental sighs or grimaces might accompany the watching, placing the child in the painful position of not being able to gain parental approval if he does what he really wants to. Children want their parent's love and approval. Whenever love and approval are conditional, whether the condition is getting a high score in a maths test, eating green vegetables, or watching only parentally condoned television shows, there is coercion.

People new to the idea of non-coercive parenting often insist that whilst they can see the value of non-coercion in most cases, there must surely be extreme occasions in which coercion is necessary, if not valuable. What constitutes these 'extreme occasions' is quite variable. For some, coercion is necessary to solve a case of head lice; for others it is reserved for tooth brushing; still others insist that it is the default position in situations where medication seems to be necessary. There is no consensus among parents about what issues are so important that they require coercion, though they will often see it as 'common sense' to hold on to the notion that there must be some issue or issues in which coercion is necessary for responsible parenting.

This justification of coercion as a default position actually sabotages the whole attempt to move into a consensual paradigm.

Children cannot trust that they have moved into a non-coercive environment or that it is in their interests to join in with the process of finding common preferences if they know that the bottom line is that the parent reserves the right to coerce. In order to be willing to be open-minded and available to the possibility of change, children need to be confident that they do not have to come up with a solution that fits into the parental notion of necessary action. If we coerce by mistake, children will understand our humanity and fallibility. If we coerce because we reserve the right when all else fails, we are stuck with conventional parenting - perhaps towards the liberal end, but not radically different in the final analysis.

Another common response to coercion is to want to redefine certain coercive behaviours as 'not really coercive'. Surely, changing a dirty nappy is not coercive? Surely, cajoling a child to go on a family outing is not coercive? There is a tendency to want to 'grade' coercion. Thus, acts of parental violence and abuse are put at one end, and changing nappies and insisting that a child goes to the cinema with everyone else, at the other end, in the 'not real coercion' category. It may be true that certain things do more damage than others, but this attempt to grade coercion is fraught with problems. None of us can second-guess the precise effects of any one thing on a particular mind. Rather than wasting energy on this futile grading exercise, we would do better to stay with the simple definition of coercion. Anything that is done against the child's will, anything that causes the child to do or think x while he still wants to do or think y, is coercion. Coercing runs the risk of causing damage and puts us in the immoral position of compromising the autonomy of another human being and is best avoided.

There is perhaps one caveat that is worth mentioning. A common rejoinder is that surely we would coerce our child to save his life. We would, for example, pull our child out of the path of a speeding lorry without first trying to reach a common preference in the micro-second available to us. Yes, we would! This is not coercion unless we knew that the child had a well-thought-out death wish and had deliberately jumped after, say, establishing that his rare disease was not and never would be susceptible to any medical treatment. In nearly all cases of children narrowly escaping car injuries or death, the child wants to live. Within a couple of seconds of being pulled back from the road, the child will gladly accept the parent's reasoning for grabbing him and will be happy to be shown safer ways to cross or achieve his actual goal in that moment. There is no real conflict in the child's mind, provided he can still get to whatever was calling him to the other side of the road, so there is no coercion.

This example actually happens rarely and it is not a justification for coercing in situations where time is pressurised because of bad planning or lack of foresight. A doctor's appointment does not have the same emergency status as a speeding truck, no matter how much parents may sometimes be tempted to make it seem like that.

Rationality

True education is about gaining knowledge in those areas in which one wants to gain knowledge. It is about learning those things that are interesting and useful to the individual concerned. We are most likely to achieve that when we proceed rationally. Rational thinking is about genuinely searching for the truth. To accomplish this, there must be the possibility of refutation as well as conjecture, and openness to criticism both from oneself and from the theories of others. This means that others, particularly parents, cannot appeal to their superior authority or experience or to their adherence to bodies of so-called authoritative thinking or belief on a particular subject in order to short circuit the process. Rational argument should speak for itself and be willing to give way to new and better theories. Rational interactions play a crucial role in reaching solutions that work for all the parties concerned - in other words, in reaching common preferences.

There is often a tendency to believe that reasoning is something that develops with maturity and experience, and is dependent on our ability to construct an articulate argument. This kind of thinking allows that we can 'reason' with older children according to their age and developing intellectual capacity, but not with babies, toddlers and young children who are pre-verbal or have more limited articulacy and logic. Being rational and being able to reason are not the same thing as having a certain level of articulacy, intellectual development or leverage through verbal logic. A baby constantly creates new knowledge and as such is a rational being. We can find common preferences with any rational being. We may not always use words. We may sometimes use very simple words with visual and practical demonstration, but we will definitely be aware of a baby or toddler's preference. We can also clearly see that toddlers and babies are able to move to new preferences or (in their own way), suggest new solutions to adults.

It is sometimes assumed that if finding common preferences is a rational process then it must be acceptable to employ this process to coerce a child who is deemed to be acting irrationally. This is not the case. It may be true that a child's thinking has been damaged by coercion and so in certain areas a child may be acting irrationally. This damage does not justify further immoral intrusion into the child's autonomy. Adding more potential damage through more coercion is not a solution. Even more importantly, it is very hard, if not impossible, to look into another mind. We cannot say with any degree of certainty whether behaviours are the result of irrationality caused by coercion damage or if they might actually be very good theories which deserve our consideration but, because of *our own* irrationality, we find them hard to follow. Getting into such psychological guessing games is both futile and destructive. We do far better simply to meet each theory with criticism and creativity, without pejorative and dismissive labels.

Fallibility

One of the things that assist non-coercive parents is recognition of their own fallibility. If we take seriously the possibility that we might be wrong then we are much less likely to attempt to force our view onto another, even when we strongly believe that it is correct. Fallibility is central to the pursuance of rational discourse in parenting and education. Our theories may well be right, but we can never know that as an absolute certainty. We should always be open to the possibility that the other has a better theory.

Creativity

Another crucial element in finding common preferences is creativity. Creativity is simply the ability to problem solve in ways that create new knowledge, resulting in new theories which are useful and relevant to the participants. The problem being solved does not have to be unpleasant; it is merely the presenting state or condition that one wants to move or grow from. Creativity is the ability to move from one state of mind to a preferred state of mind.

People new to TCS sometimes object that not everyone can be creative and that they do not see themselves as having creativity and so are likely to be set up to fail before they even start. This is not what is meant by creativity within the TCS philosophy. As the website entry on this subject puts it:

*"This is to misunderstand what we mean by 'creativity'.
Building a satisfying life is itself a creative endeavour.
Developing good moral theories is a creative endeavour ...
Creativity plays a part in all improvement in each and every
area of life. Coercion impairs creativity. This is not limited to
the narrow sphere, which is often called creativity....*

*"Being creative depends on being able to recognise useful and
relevant conjectures. But it depends on even more than that.
For instance, there is the matter of being able to create or
recognise useful and relevant problems. And the ability to
invent or recognise, and apply, powerful methods of criticism.
And the ability to discard theories that fail to survive criticism,
and to re-adjust one's background knowledge so as to reveal
new and better problems."*

(TCS website: www.tcs.ac
copyright (1997-99) Sarah Lawrence)

Criticism

Along the way, rationality and creativity are aided by criticism.
That is not to say that negative demeaning of another's argument,
particularly the dismissive criticism of a child's argument by a
parent, is likely to help the growth of knowledge. Taking the other's
theory seriously, however, and engaging with it to point out
perceived problems makes a genuine contribution, especially when
there is no compulsion to accept the criticism.

Theories

The TCS philosophy uses the word 'theory' very broadly to indicate
any state of mind, or being, or disposition, that is active within a
given person. The TCS website defines theory as:

*"... any of the following: aspect of personality, assumption,
behavioural tendency, belief, concept, conception, conjecture,
conviction, deduction, desire, disposition, ethical maxim,
expectation, explanation, fear, gene, guess, habit, hope,
hypothesis, idea, impression, impulse, inspiration, mental
image, meme, mental picture, meta-theory, notion, opinion,
postulate, predisposition, premise, presumption, pre-
supposition, psychological characteristic, psychological
tendency, rationale, sensation, skill, speculation, state of mind,
supposition, surmise, suspicion, theory, thought, trait, etc."*

(TCS website, www.tcs.ac
copyright TCS (1997-99) Sarah Lawrence)

Theories can be conscious or unconscious, explicit, inexplicit, inborn, inherited or learnt; but none are immutable. Some of our theories are deeply entrenched. They are not open to rational criticism or subject to creative problem solving, but are so strongly held that no reason can effect them.

Let us go back to Jane. After a lifetime of coercion - all in the name of her own good and best interest - Jane grows up and becomes a parent. She is now convinced that children need to be taught to sleep for certain amounts of time to keep them healthy. Her baby has other ideas, and months, if not years, of conflict and misery follow while Jane imposes her 'essential' routine. Jane has become incapable of thinking openly and rationally about the area of sleep. No amount of reason or criticism is going to convince Jane that her baby's brain and health do not require an imposed sleep regime. Jane's friends offer other good ideas. Jane can see that they have a certain logic to them. She can see that her friends' children do not appear to be suffering from sleep deprivation, despite a great variety of patterns, but she still cannot bring herself to let go of her fear that without a controlled regime her baby will suffer. Jane's theories are entrenched.

Common preferences

A key feature of any family following a consent-based philosophy is the practice of finding common preferences. This is simply any solution to any problem that all the participants agree to be preferable to either their original solutions or to any other solutions that have been considered. A common preference implies a win-win situation in which everyone is pleased with the outcome. It is not a compromise in which one solution wins whilst others give way, reluctantly or sadly or with the poor option that they will get their turn to win another time. Common preferences rely on genuine consent. They also rely on the ability of the participants to change their original preference during the process of problem solving. This does not mean that original preferences are never followed. Sometimes the original preference of one person may turn out to be the common preference of all, but unless there is a basic willingness to change and explore new ideas then no common preference can be reached. Finding mutually desired solutions demands both rationality and creativity and the basic belief that solutions do exist to problems, even if we do not always find them.

Within families, we are not used to win-win scenarios with everyone on the same side. We are used to assuming that often, if not always, someone must lose; that compromise is about as good as it gets, and that conflict is inevitable. TCS challenges these very basic parenting assumptions. It is not utopian. It is not an elite parenting school for perfect people or for parents chronically addicted to sacrificing themselves to their monstrously demanding children. Common preferences work. They work in large and small families, poor and rich families, families from every cultural and ethnic background, families with and without adherence to particular faiths, families with one parent or two parents or gay parents or living in communities. Common preferences work wherever there is a fundamental trust that children are rational and creative. Wherever there is the essential realism to admit that we are all fallible and therefore need to proceed on every issue with an open mind, wherever we are willing to devote our time, energy, and resources to consent, instead of to conflict and damage, **then** everyone can win.

Common preferences also require another basic assumption. If we assume that a child getting what she wants is a bad thing, and if we believe that a child having his desires, wants, needs and theories taken seriously to the extent of finding solutions that the child always prefers, is a corrupting indulgence, then we are not likely to be able to enter into the process of finding common preferences. In order to enter into the process of finding common preferences with our children, we have to believe that 'what they want' is not inimical to or the opposite of moral living and caring about others. Children expressing their preferences are simply doing the right thing for themselves, which may very well be the thing that also has great benefits for others as well. Why should we think that, given autonomy, our children would choose evil? It is a fear that is false and which needs questioning at every turn (and an issue to which we will return).

A new paradigm

Amongst liberal parenting theories there is a wide variety which would claim to take children seriously. What this often means is listening to children and taking account of children's views, but without necessarily giving them equal weight and with no commitment not to coerce the children in the final decision. Only TCS philosophy goes further than this. It proposes a whole new paradigm for interaction between parents and children, to reach solutions in which children's autonomy and right not to be coerced is fully respected. It is a paradigm that tends to evoke strong responses and a barrage of questions. Is it not likely to lead to neglect? What if the child wants to engage in all sorts of dangerous or immoral behaviours? Surely the parents end up as slaves to every childish whim with no time or energy to do what they want in their own lives? These and many other questions will be explored in the following chapters. What is important to assert from the outset is that TCS is an eminently practical philosophy precisely because every family tailors it to their own lifestyle and preferences. It is also, I believe, the only theory of parenting and education which fosters truly autonomous education since it places the emphasis squarely on the child's intrinsic motivation and does not fall prey to the lure of products and outcomes.

For those of us who have already taken the step of putting our children's autonomy centre stage in their education, particularly within the home-education community, the realisation that life will never be the same again is generally not slow in dawning on us. Valuing educational autonomy soon leads to massive shifts in lifestyle. I am convinced that it is only TCS that adequately answers the lifestyle and parenting questions, which arise from a commitment to autonomous education. TCS is not, however, exclusively the preserve of home-educating parents. There are many for whom the need to find alternative parenting practices which eradicate the stress of continual conflict and uneasy compromise from their lives come before any consideration of educational theory. The chapters that follow will, I hope, be of equal value however the approach is made. One thing is certain; life with TCS will challenge every assumption you have ever made.

Chapter two

The parental role

The theory of non-coercive parenting often elicits in people's minds an image of laissez-faire or even neglectful parenting. This is not the case. The parental role in a TCS family is highly engaged and interactive, but coercion is not an option within those interactions. TCS parents give up all notions of parental domination and authority, but not of parental responsibility.

In this chapter I will look at the role of the parent in fostering autonomy and intrinsically motivated learning. I will consider issues such as the parent as a repository for morality and source of advice, information, and criticism and how these roles can be made consistent with non-coercion. I will look at the process of finding mutually desired solutions and the place of parents' wider access to life experience whilst abandoning the conventional notions that parents 'know best' or have a duty to coerce 'for the child's own good.' This chapter will look at the difficulties of overcoming parental entrenched theories, and highlight the pitfalls for autonomy and education of conflating non-coercive parenting with either of the blind alleys of laissez-faire parenting or self-sacrifice. I will begin by looking at the issues of inequality of power and responsibility in the child-parent relationship.

A non-symmetrical relationship

Parents have more power than do children. This power is boosted by the natural desire of children to want their parents' approval and liking. Parents decide to have children. The children have no say in this and do not enter into any form of contract to obey the parent merely by the act of being born. Parents, on the other hand, do have a moral obligation towards their children. They are obliged to care for and help their children. This does not mean that taking children seriously is merely a matter of 'giving way'; rather, it is a matter of finding common preferences with the child. It is only in the event of the failure of the process of finding common preferences that a parent should 'give way'. In reality there are always solutions out there (the theoretical possibility of a solution), but we do not always find it. We are, however, more likely to find solutions the more we practice using our creativity in this way.

The trusted advisor

So, the parent has moral responsibility to care for and help the child, but not to coerce the child. What role does this leave in practice? Aside from the obvious issues of providing shelter, food and clothing, the parent becomes a repository for morality and a source of advice, information and criticism. It is a misconception to equate non-coercion with never telling our children what are our own moral views of right and wrong. Living consensually does not mean that we should never make suggestions about information, activities, foods or anything else. It does not mean keeping our advice to ourselves, unless the child has heard it a hundred times and asks us to refrain from repeating it. Sharing our theories is an important - in fact, vital - parental role.

All that we can share are our own best theories. These may be very good or they may, in fact, be completely fallacious. Sharing them will be a good thing as long as we accept our own fallibility and do not expect sharing to lead to compliance. We can even share theories about things which are highly personal - hair colour, bodily odour, room tidiness - provided that we are prepared to accept that in the final analysis some things are simply a matter of bodily autonomy. If we would not expect an adult friend to comply, then we have no right to expect compliance from a child. Of course, Judy may be quite happy to delay dyeing her hair green until after Grandma's visit and Ben might welcome the tips about personal hygiene before his first date, in which case there is a common preference. If we are willing to acknowledge our own fallibility and if we are able to restrain ourselves from insisting, even when we are very sure that we are right, then our children are most likely to learn to look upon us as trusted advisors. They will realise that we are not omniscient and sometimes speak unadulterated rubbish. Despite this, they will still be more than willing to ask for our opinion - to hear us out, to engage with our ideas, to listen to and weigh up our criticisms - if they know that they can do so without fear of coercion or loss of autonomy.

The trusted advisor role is highly active and engaged. When it is working well and our children really trust that it will not lead to coercion, it is likely that parents will be given far more access to their children's lives than conventional parents would have. After all, saying 'no' on principal and holding on to parental authority and threatening punishment have no proven track record of keeping children safe; but rather, these methods constitute a well-recognised reason for children resorting to lying or secretly engaging in dangerous behaviour without any advice.

Mutual solutions

Sharing theories whilst avoiding coercion and eschewing the conventional wisdom of punishment is not only a point of morality and a parenting issue; it is also an educational matter. Insistence that our theories should be followed and the possibility of punishment or consequences, however 'liberally' conceived, damages the child's ability to think rationally and openly about the subject in hand. How can a child listen to rational arguments about drugs, (which stand on their own merits and have the force of rational persuasion), if she really knows that ultimately the decision will be forced from her, or she will have to resort to deception? How can a child decide that eating nothing but pop tarts may effect his health, if he is prevented from weighing the information and conducting his own further enquiries by a threat that if he does not desist no more pop tarts will be bought? Either the information and theories are good enough to stand on their merits, or they are not. Either the parent will be convincing, or it will be seen in the process of discussion that more information is needed, or that the child has a better theory, or that it is not a theory that has universal application, but simply a matter of taste and choice.

Our theories, information, moral views and criticisms are gifts which we give to our children - not merely because it is morally beholden on us as part of parental responsibility, but because we care deeply about them. We have no corresponding moral duty to impose our theories on them. It is ultimately for the recipient to make best use of the gift by his or her own lights.

Coercion and protection

This is equally the case when the issue is one in which the parent feels the child needs protection. It is not right to act immorally by thwarting someone's will in order to achieve the supposedly good end of protecting them. Whether the protection is physical or verbal, it still requires that a common preference be found. Parents sometimes object that they have a very much greater pool of life experiences to draw on. This can lead them to believe that wider access to life experience allows them to insist that parents 'know best' or have a duty to coerce 'for the child's own good'. This is not the case. Parents undoubtedly have more experience than children. This will have led them to form some very good theories. It will also have immersed them in conventional parental thinking about children, have exposed them to a lifetime of being coerced themselves, and fostered in them a whole range of entrenched and faulty thinking. Experience offers one form of input, but it is not necessarily rational. Offering experience with acknowledgement of our fallibility is a far cry from deciding that we know best. Furthermore, children, although they lack experience, have sustained less coercion damage, on average, than adults and can often proffer very good rational criticism.

Another situation in which parents are tempted to intervene coercively with their own theories 'on behalf' of their children, is when the children themselves are considering entering a coercive environment. This might be a fundamentalist Sunday school class teaching creationism; a classroom controlled by mechanical rules; a rule-bound sports training session; or a uniformed organisation with the motto 'Seek, Serve and Follow'. These are not environments that would most readily spring to mind in connection with young people from TCS homes. They are all places where they are likely to encounter attempts at coercion and where the theories that they hear at home are likely to be strongly criticised. In many cases, children will choose to avoid such environments as being fraught with difficulties, but in other cases a child will choose such an environment despite its coercive ethos for good reasons of his or her own. When this happens, non-coercive parents can sometimes be worried that their children will suffer damage from the coercion inherent within the chosen environment, or that their child will adopt theories which the parents themselves find inferior.

Neither of these worries need be entertained if the home itself is truly non-coercive. Consider the example of the Sunday school. A relatively young child decides that this is a good place to hear stories and meet with other children. All goes well for a while, until the teacher begins to expound his ideas about creationism. The child counters with theories he has discussed at home and has accepted as valid. The child's arguments naturally cut no ice, as the teacher's views are not open to rational criticism and are not falsifiable. Instead, the child is informed that it is wicked not to accept the theory (or rather, dogma) of creationism and is left with the definite impression that he must accept the dogma if he is to maintain the approval of the teacher. If the child comes from a home where coercion is normal, then it is likely that a high degree of damage will occur. The child will be used to seeking approval as something that must be earned. If his parents disagree with the Sunday school teacher and are keen for the child to share their understanding of evolution, he could lose parental approval by switching allegiance to his teacher's views and vice versa. The child will not make a rational decision about best theories or his own interests, but a coerced one in which internal loyalties conflict.

On the other hand, a child from a non-coercive home will not be placed in this appalling dilemma. A non-coerced child will have the secure knowledge that he is acceptable for himself and does not have to jump through any hoops to retain this acceptability at home. If he is pressured to conform in another environment, he knows that he can rely on his parents' advocacy and that any lack of acceptance on his teacher's part is the teacher's problem and not the child's. The non-coerced child will choose a theory on its own merits with a rational appraisal, knowing that he does not risk parental disapproval and that his well being is not dependent on his teacher's approval.

Take the example of the classroom. Many children, used to being taken seriously, would avoid this environment as one unlikely to contribute to their own growth of knowledge and access to fun. A child, however, might very well have her own reasons for choosing to take part in a school environment. The coercion which schools are normally able to exert depends, to a large degree, on parental collusion with the coercive system. A child who knows that she can end the relationship with school at any time and who knows she will be supported over issues such as not doing homework will have a totally different experience of school than the child who has not entered the environment on her own volition.

In short, it is not any particular environment in itself that can inflict coercion damage, even when coercion is an overt feature of the environment. Rather, it is a question of information and expectation. Conflicting information, when it is offered without pressure, will create no conflicts. When expectation enters into the equation, however, then coercion comes with it. Such expectation can be extremely damaging not only in its most overt forms, but also when it is employed with more subtlety. A parent may not directly express disappointment in a child's decision to utilise a potentially coercive environment; but there are many ways of expressing this disappointment through such looks, sighs, and/or negative asides that can put the child into a state of conflict.

Imagine, for example, a mother who believes that certain TV programmes 'coerce' her children into holding certain opinions that she finds distasteful. She also believes in not being coercive towards her children, so she none the less allows her children to watch the offending programs. The children only 'choose' to do so when she is out of the house, knowing, as they do, how offended she is by such 'rubbish'. In such a scenario, information is being communicated in an expectation-laden manner. The mother shares her best theory; but more than that, she shares it repeatedly and is unwilling to consider the possibility that her theory may be wrong. She then adds expectation into this situation. Although she overtly tells her children that they 'may' watch whatever they please, she uses subtle communication to make them have to choose between their own theory and her approval. They can do whatever they want, but must not expect to still be approved of, or to be able to watch without feeling uncomfortable.

TCS parents have their best theories and a wealth of experience and information, and it is only right that they should fully share this with their children. There have to be expectation-free ways of communicating that information, however, if coercion is to be avoided. It is quite natural for children to want to please their parents and for them to desire parental approval. Such approval should be a given and not a condition of adopting certain theories or using only certain pre-approved environments. It is equally natural that parents should want to protect their children and that they might be anxious about the potential coercion that certain situations might exert over their children.

Parents would be remiss if they did not warn their children about this hazard and discuss ways of avoiding possible coercion. They will become part of that coercion only if they attempt in any way to ensure that there can be only one outcome. Information shared fully and frankly is a vital part of the parent-child interaction. Expectation, on the other hand, introduces a desire to manipulate someone else's mind and has no part in consensual relationships.

Parental entrenched theories

This brings us to the difficulty of overcoming parental entrenched theories. We all have areas in which our theories are very poor indeed, often because of the coercion we have experienced ourselves. Entrenched theories are those theories which are not open to rational criticism or subject to creative problem solving, but which are so strongly held that reason seems unable to affect them.

Peter, for example, is a father who is trying to live without coercing his family. Despite some early misgivings he has found it relatively easy to let go of control of television and bedtimes. He struggled more when it came to food, holding deep convictions that those he cares about should eat only organic, vegetarian food. He has worked on this issue with his children. After false starts, mistakes and apologies, he has come to see that not only are his children right to claim their bodily autonomy, but that they have some very good criticisms of his food theories which are now affecting his own eating habits.

Another problem for Peter is that he simply cannot abide mess. He is quite happy to clean the kitchen and living room each day. It does not take too long and it gives him places where he can relax and eat according to his own comfort levels. He does not expect his children to help with this, but sometimes they do join in and give a hand. This is not enough for Peter. He wants his children to have tidy rooms. His arguments are met with very good counter arguments; 'This is my personal space', 'I know where everything is even if it looks like chaos', 'Mum has no problem collecting underwear off the floor once a week and I don't mind her coming in for that', 'Nothing has ever been broken because of the mess', 'My friends don't mind, their rooms are just the same', 'I've never gone down with some terrible disease as the result of the odd mouldy cup and plate lying on the floor', and so on. Peter acknowledges that all of these arguments 'seem' convincing, but he still simply cannot abide the thought of the mess. Whenever he sees into his son's room, he feels overwhelmingly angry; yet he insists that his son, Daniel, is the one who is being irrational. Surely every rational person wants to live in tidiness? Surely Daniel's' intransigence is simply unreasonable?

No, it is not. Daniel has put forward good reasons and at the end of the day this is his room. He should have the deciding say in how to organise his personal space. That is not to say that Daniel should not work on some common preferences. It makes sense to get clothes into the laundry and pots into the dishwasher, but he has already thought of this and found some solutions. If Daniel were simply being unreasonable, then he probably would not have reached this working solution. The problem is Peter's, so what can he do?

There is nothing wrong with Peter continuing to seek common preferences with Daniel. They share the same house and it is in their common interest to feel comfortable. If Peter, however, finds that he is simply making the same suggestions (or even demands) repeatedly, then Daniel is unlikely to want to go on hearing them. It seems much more likely that the intransigence is on Peter's side. He is the one who is stuck on an idea that he really cannot justify, but simply 'feels' to be the case. Probably the best thing they can do is to leave the issue alone for a while. Perhaps Daniel might agree to keeping his door shut so that Peter is less likely to notice how it looks and less likely to experience irrational anger. Perhaps they can agree not to talk about this for a while. When Peter is feeling able to face the issue again, perhaps he could begin by talking to other TCS parents and getting lots of ideas on tidiness and mess. Entrenched theories are not immutable, but they often need several bouts of work and periods of desisting before new theories emerge.

Laissez-faire parenting does not take children seriously

TCS parents have a primary role in their children's lives, yet many people, on first considering the theory, fall into the misconception of conflating autonomy and non-coercive parenting with laissez-faire parenting. TCS does not condone neglect, however dressed up in liberal philosophy. Abandoning children to their own devices without the constant input of information, moral beliefs and the gift of criticism is a failure of parental duty. Laissez-faire parenting is simply a liberal form of coercion in that children are denied access to parental care and help. Not making the final decision about what another human being puts into his body, is not the same as not offering our theories about nutrition, or offering to do internet searches with the child on diet, or taking the child to lots of different eating establishments so that he can have fun experimenting with taste. Giving our children privacy is not the same as ignoring them for several years. Helping our children to learn about food preparation because this is one of their areas of interest is not a reason never to cook for them. TCS parents are very engaged parents. They do not simply 'leave their offspring to it'; they ensure that their children have what they need to make well-informed decisions about their lives.

Self-sacrifice

If TCS is not being accused of being laissez-faire, then it is likely that it is being targeted as encouraging parental self-sacrifice. The logic is that if our children are getting what they want out of life, then surely they can be doing so only at our expense? This is based on the false, but common, assumption that parents and children are always in some way opposed and competing and that 'win-win' situations exist only in fairy stories. This assumption is wrong. What we are aiming at is consensual living. There cannot be full consent when one or more parties, in this case the parents, are unhappy with the solution. Not coercing our children does not mean becoming doormats with no lives. In fact, people generally find that when they begin eradicating coercion from their relationships with their children, they are also less willing to live with coercion in other areas of their lives. The adults are likely to begin expecting to be able to have their needs and wants met too.

It is the case, however, that TCS parents believe that in the event that no common preference is found, it is better to self-sacrifice than to coerce. This is a failure. It is something to be reflected on and improved upon. It happens because we lack creativity in the moment, perhaps because we are too tired or stressed or have made mistakes in setting the situation up or are dealing with an area where we have faulty thinking or entrenched theories. It is more likely to happen when we first begin to try to live without coercion or when we are encountering an issue that we have not previously dealt with non-coercively. It is not a good solution. It is a poor default, one that should be used less and less as we become practised at creative problem solving.

Why is it a bad solution? After all, parents are used to the notion that parenting is a sacrificial activity and self-sacrifice is often ennobled by society. Self-sacrifice is a bad solution because it robs the participants in any problem-solving scenario of genuine solutions. When a common preference is found, everyone has continued working until all the participants are genuinely pleased with the outcome. This creative activity produces new knowledge and enlarges the family's thinking. If, at some stage of the process, the parent simply abandons their own desires, then they are robbing the family of ideas and creative input. If this pattern continues, rather than being an occasional occurrence, which is acknowledged as a failure, then no one in the family will become practised in finding common preferences. In place of win-win solutions, there will be the prevailing conventional notion that someone has to lose. The only difference is that now the parent is the loser instead of the child. We do not increase our children's ability to think and problem-solve creatively by constantly stunting the creative process. We do not show either our children or ourselves that win-win solutions are possible by agreeing to lose each time. Furthermore, we are likely to build up resentment towards our children if we continually self-sacrifice. This can often result in an explosion of coercion when the sacrificial victim can stand it no longer, with an ensuing loss of trust in the whole common preference finding process.

The TCS parent

So how can we sum up the role of the TCS parent? TCS parents recognise that they have a moral duty to care for, support, and help their children, and are conscious that this is not a reciprocal contract that involves an obligation of obedience on the part of the child. TCS parents are highly engaged with their children's lives, though always with respect to the child's wishes in any given area. They are parents who are fully available to their children and happy to share their theories. They also recognise their own fallibility and respect the child's autonomy. In this way, TCS parents become trusted advisors to whom children can turn to for honest criticism and rational debate without fear of coercion. These parents recognise that they themselves have entrenched theories, and so are prepared to desist when the occasion demands. Despite this, they are not laissez-faire parents or advocates of self-sacrifice, but rather, finders of common preferences. They are parents who will go to great lengths to assist their children. They are prepared to challenge every assumption, but they are not prepared to coerce. Why? Because coercion is damaging.

Chapter three

Non-coercion and the growth of knowledge

Non-coercive parenting assumes that real learning is intrinsic learning and must, therefore, be based around satisfying preferences. In this chapter, I will look in more detail at how coercion can derail this process, and note that the effects of coercion can be damaging even when we are unable to predict those effects with any accuracy. I will examine how coercion leads to entrenched thinking, thus effectively shutting down the learning process. I will also look at arguments that coercion damage can be used to justify further coercion and as a basis for forming limiting theories about our children; I contend that these positions are false and detrimental. Having established that coercion damages thinking and that theorising about our children simply places limits around the growth of their knowledge, I will move on to examine the role of reason in the growth of knowledge. I will also consider the roles of intrinsically motivated learning and self-interest in the growth of knowledge.

More about coercion damage

It is a fundamental premise of this book that coercion damages thinking ability and rationality. When we choose coercion over finding a common preference, we not only lose the possibility of new knowledge being created, but also risk impairing our ability to think, learn, and solve problems. In situations where there is a problem to be solved, coerced children will abandon the attempt creatively to problem solve, knowing it to be futile since ultimately the solution will be imposed by the adults. Learning does not take place and creativity is trampled. Children need to have successful experiences of finding solutions and having control over their own lives. Coercion replaces this experience with feelings of powerlessness, resentment, and frustration, adding painful feelings to areas of thinking and another blockage to rational thinking. Coercion helps to convince children that life is difficult, that getting what one wants is next to impossible and that doing things one hates in inevitable; non-coercion creates flexible thinkers who see that they can control their lives, and develop lives which they want to live.

Positing that coercion does damage is not the same as being able accurately to predict what that damage will be in each case. Every person is affected uniquely. Damage will affect different areas of lives and thinking, and each individual will have his or her own kind of resilience in the face of coercion. In some way, the ability to problem-solve in one or more areas will be impaired. Clear thinking is likely to give way to irrationality, which might exhibit itself as fearfulness, anger when certain topics are raised, repression, or gross sensitivities, (for example).

Humans are born to learn. Intrinsic learning and coercion are inimical. TCS parents are in the business of helping their children to satisfy their preferences and pursue their intrinsically motivated learning in every direction. Coercive parents, on the other hand, have a fixed idea of what learning they want their children to do. This agenda sabotages attempts to pursue learning that is not parentally sanctioned. If learning is categorised as 'appropriate' or 'inappropriate', children will either abandon their attempts to have their preferences taken seriously or develop a range of sophisticated coping strategies. Their original preferences can get lost in a maze of subterfuge. They can become adults who are scarcely aware of what their preferences for their own lives are; who are almost certainly convinced that even if they know what they want, they cannot have it.

People sometimes object that they know of many children whose parents employ coercion and many adults who were coerced as children who are nevertheless bright, successful, intelligent people. This might be true, but it does not mean that the coercion they experienced did no damage. It might be that the bright, intelligent person is none the less very poor at forming relationships or has irrational thinking difficulties when it comes to washing dishes or cannot bear to be disagreed with. Some people may be much more resilient to the effects of coercion than others, but this does not justify coercion. As parents, we cannot predict what damage any particular act of coercion will do. What we can predict is that at some point, in some areas and to some degree, coercion will cause thinking damage. We can also cogently hold that all coercion has the potential to cause damage. Why damage our children? The usual reason is that we are committing some minor bad for some greater good; that we are limiting our children's preferences out of their own best interests. This reasoning is false and we will return to it in chapter six.

One of the indicators of coercion damage is the prevalence of entrenched theories. These are theories which are held intransigently and which seem impervious to rational discussion or change. They severely limit the growth of knowledge and sabotage mutually agreed solutions in family life. A regular question from people new to TCS concerns what to do in the face of children who refuse to take part in problem solving. This is a difficult and fraught area for someone who is trying to make a radical switch in their parenting style. It can help to remember that adding more coercion to an already damaged situation is not going to help the situation improve. It is unlikely that parents will find their children unwilling to engage in problem solving in any area at all, so it might be helpful to back away from difficult areas and highlight the progress and success that the family is making in other areas. As children come to trust the process and to see that common preferences can be found, they are more likely to be willing to begin seeking creative solutions in more and more areas of their life.

In many cases, however, the problem is the other way round. Children often find the process of common preferences one that they can adopt very quickly, whilst the parent finds that, despite his or her best efforts, there are certain areas in which they can hardly bear to think about non-coercion. Getting support from other people who have encountered similar blocks can be very helpful. Sometimes the parent simply needs to back off from the specific area and allow the theory and practice of non-coercion to become more deeply ingrained in his or her lifestyle before the child can approach the issue again. Most people find that, as they go on living in this radical new paradigm, deeper and deeper areas of entrenched thinking will surface to be dealt with. There begins a lifelong process of moving from entrenched to open thinking.

Theorising about our children

We all, adults and children alike, have areas in which our thinking is damaged by coercion, where we act irrationally or our theories are entrenched. This knowledge can tempt parents to discount certain theories which their children propose, on the basis that they are saying x, or proposing to act in y way, only because they are coercion damaged and irrational. This is a dangerous trap to fall into. Attempting to trace in detail the effects of coercion damage or precisely to define or label areas of irrationality is likely to impede our non-coercive dealings with children, and to belittle them rather than take them seriously.

The tendency to make theories about our children is one of the easiest errors to fall into. A distant aunt or enquiring stranger might, in casual conversation, expect that we will be able to rattle off a list of our children's defining attributes in order to fix them in their mind: 'Jane is a tomboy', 'Alan is rather hyperactive', 'Joe has reading difficulties', 'Louise is a maths genius'. The trouble with these theories is that they define the child as a static product, implying that this is what or who the child is and ever shall be. Furthermore, they fix the child according to someone else's outside observations and subjective perceptions. The person, often a parent, might spend a lot of time with the child, be very engaged with the child and know the child well by any conventional measure. Even so, there is still an overlay of theory that is always external and open to being faulty.

The problem for parents is that in order to help our children get what they want, we feel it will assist us if we know what kind of person it is that we are helping. Are not we more likely to make appropriate suggestions that our children will prefer if we have a handy thumb nail picture of John, who is an outgoing extrovert, who loves to be always on the move, has lots of energy, is not very patient?

Conventional liberal parenting would say, *"Yes, you will be a more helpful parent if you know your child's personality type, know what makes him tick, have the right labels for any disabilities or learning problems"*, and so forth. This is not taking children seriously. Children are individuals. If we begin to treat someone according to a packaged personality type, we are not treating them as a unique and constantly changing individual, but with the gross disrespect of someone who really cannot be bothered to attend to that unique person at that moment. I am not saying that we can know nothing about our children, or that we must begin every engagement as though we were starting from scratch. That would waste time and knowledge. What we must be aware of, though, is the kind of knowledge we have and how best to use it.

We constantly make observations about one another - 'Each time we go to town Jane wants to visit the Barbie section of the toy shop', 'Jane spends a lot of time drawing figures of girls', 'Jane likes experimenting with make up and jewellery.' These observations are fine as long as we do not fall into the trap of having a fixed idea about what Jane will do or want on every future occasion. We should not, for example, start channelling Jane down pre-set routes that fit in with our perceptions and observations. Rather, we should be tentative about the suggestions we make based on our observations. We do not let our observations become fixed theories. I may observe Jane very often and spend a lot of time with Jane, but I am still not Jane. No matter how much time we spend together, we never know what is going on inside someone else's head. Our observations can only ever be of a tiny portion of the learning and thinking and developing within Jane. By all means, suggest more visits to the shops with Barbies, suggest buying Barbies, provide access to lots of make up and jewellery and paper and drawing mediums, think of lots of creative ways to add to the delight Jane takes in all these things. At the same time, be open to the loves of today being dropped tomorrow, or going off in new and previously un-thought-of directions. Above all, do not conclude that Jane is 'a very feminine little girl', 'into all the girly things', 'bound to grow up to be a model or a make-up artist', 'rather empty headed', 'a bit on the frivolous side', 'too obsessed with the trivial', 'in danger of developing warped views of women's bodies', 'in need of more balanced interests' or any one of a hundred other theories that fix a child according to someone else's agenda and are likely to interfere with the intrinsic learning which is taking place.

Once we step back and admit that we are all subjective observers who are fallible and liable to employ our own overlay of perceptions, then we can become more tentative about how we employ our observations and less likely to do damage with them. Consider Jason, an eleven-year-old who does not exhibit fluent literacy to the observing world. His parents also observe that Jason has a lot of energy and appears (to them), to be often frustrated and destructive. In many conventional homes, Jason would be only a hair's breadth away from being diagnosed with 'Attention Deficit Hyperactivity Disorder', medicated with ritalin, labelled as having a specific learning difficulty and plugged into a remedial reading programme. Theorising about Jason leads to seeing him not as a unique person, but as a certain category of child for whom a certain package of solutions can be prescribed. These labels will fix Jason and this 'fixing' will derail his own intrinsic learning processes.

What is the alternative? Firstly, instead of forming theories about our children, we can take a breath and stop at our observations. If we admit that what we have are tentative, subjective observations, which are open to refutation or revision, then we are much less likely to do any damage. 'I observe that Jason is not reading fluently at the moment.' 'I observe that Jason has broken several things around the home this week when he has appeared angry.' 'I observe that Jason is frustrated by being woken up in the mornings/told to brush his teeth.' These are our observations, but that does not entitle us to impose a formula on them.

Secondly, do not waste time and energy trying to get inside Jason's mind. The route of psychobabble is not one that is concerned with negotiating the present, but one that is likely to add more confusing overlays to the given moment.

Thirdly, concentrate on what Jason wants. 'I might be wrong, but I got the idea you wanted to get into that book and had a bit of difficulty. Can I help?' 'You seem to be angry. What can I do about that?' 'You don't seem to like being woken up in the mornings. Can we find a better way of starting the day that works for you?'

Your offers and ideas may be way off the mark; but as long as they are made tentatively and your child knows that you are only putting forward opening gambits that can be taken or left in the melting pot of ideas, then even the most mistaken observations are going to do no harm. If we do not barrage Jason with fixed theories, then we are not likely to derail the whole intrinsic process of learning. Most fundamentally, we do not risk defining the child and setting up a fixed problem label or a static self-image that closes down whole areas of thinking and learning. In the case of Jason, for example, his internal breakthrough into fluent and sophisticated literacy might only have been a few days away, but the label 'late reader', or 'having a learning problem', could curtail that development and become self-fulfilling. On the other hand, a tentative observation and offer of assistance could speed up that final leap or be turned down as unnecessary.

We do not need to get right inside the minds of our children in order to help them and to create new knowledge with them. We only need to be available, observant, aware of our own fallibility and committed to discovering what Jane or Jason most prefer by their own lights at this moment. (*adapted from an article for the TCS journal, no 32.*)

The growth of knowledge is impeded by coercion, which causes thinking damage and entrenched theories, sabotaging our ability to reason. The growth of knowledge is not assisted by attempting to second-guess which areas of our children's thinking are damaged and irrational or by theorising about our children. So how does knowledge grow?

Reason and the growth of knowledge

Knowledge grows through reason. Unfortunately, for many people, that can suggest a very narrow way of working which excludes our emotions and intuition. This does not have to be the case. Just as 'theories' are defined very widely to include such things as personality, assumptions, desires, psychological characteristics, unconscious theories, inexplicit theories and even the inborn theories inherited in our DNA (see chapter 1 above), so reason can also encompass emotion and intuition. In fact all ways of problem solving, explicit and implicit, are part of our reason. The conclusions we reach - whether from logic, feeling, intuition or any other means - still need to be subjected to the process of conjecture and refutation. Knowledge grows when we hold it tentatively and critically, when we are committed to seeking the truth with a constant eye on our own fallibility.

As issues or problems arise within a family the process adopted is one of finding truth and new knowledge in that situation. This is found through reasoning in the widest sense. A solution is found when all the participants prefer a particular proposal, regardless of how it arose. It is a common preference. The solution does not have to be permanent, it is not absolute truth, but it is held until a new problem arises which requires new knowledge. We reach a new conjecture, something that appears to be true to the best of our knowledge and reasoning until we encounter some criticism which suggests otherwise and which leads us to begin the process again.

Let us take the example of Sandra. Sandra is a first-time mother who, faced with her longed-for baby, suddenly feels confused and overwhelmed. She has planned to breastfeed and intended to share her bed with her baby. Faced with the reality of the totally dependent infant she finds herself feeling angry when he cries for attention or seems to want to be held constantly and she has a longing for her own personal space which she has not felt before. She also feels adrift, as though she has no patterns for what mothering might mean for her. Her partner is supportive and helpful and has no strong feelings about Sandra having to breastfeed. Sandra wants to live consensually with her baby and she feels that the baby's unhindered preference would be for breastfeeding, but she also realises that her self-sacrifice would not be good for the baby any more than for herself. Sandra does not believe that she is thinking very clearly, but she has very strong feelings. She feels strongly that she wants to breast-feed. She also feels strongly that she wants to buy some bottles and not have to be the baby's source of nourishment. One friend tells her that to go on breast feeding would be self-sacrifice and she should stop now before it becomes the chronic pattern of the relationship with her baby. Sandra does not know what to say to her friend, but feels intuitively that this is not quite the case. What she wants is to be able to breast-feed and not feel that she is self-sacrificing. By following this half articulated intuition Sandra is subjecting her theories about what is self-sacrifice and what it means to nurture a baby to criticism and refutation. The criticism may not be of the most logical nature, but Sandra's perceptions begin to change. She begins to feel that this nurturing is not a cost or a drain or a sacrifice, but a joy and a preference. Sandra has created new knowledge.

Instruction from within

Knowledge grows when it is intrinsic to the learner. Karl Popper, whose philosophy has had a seminal effect on the TCS theory of parenting and education, proposed a new view of learning which is not based on the inductive view of learning. In *The Myth of the Framework* he wrote:

> *"The inductivist or Lamarkian approach operates with the idea of instruction from without, or from the environment. But the critical or Darwinian approach only allows instruction from within - from within the structure itself.*
>
> *"In fact, I contend that there is no such thing as instruction from without the structure, or the passive reception of a flow of information which impresses itself on our sense organs. All observations are theory-impregnated. There is no pure, disinterested, theory-free observation...*
>
> *"We do not discover new facts or new effects by copying them, or by inferring them inductively from observation, or by any other method of instruction by the environment. We use, rather, the method of trial and the elimination of error. As Ernst Gombrich says, 'making comes before matching': the*

> *active production of a new trial structure comes before its*
> *exposure to eliminating tests." (pp. 8-9)*

On such a theory, extrinsic motivation is ruled out as an effective strategy for learning. Instead, Popper puts problem solving at the heart of learning:

> *" The proper answer to my question 'How can we hope to*
> *detect and eliminate error?' seems to me to be 'By criticising*
> *the theories and conjectures of others and - if we can train*
> *ourselves to do so - by criticising our own theories and*
> *speculative attempts to solve problems'."*
> *(In Search of a Better World,* p.48)

Self-interest and the growth of knowledge

For knowledge to grow, self-interest functions as both an educational principle and a proper foundation for parenting. We are not accustomed to thinking about parenting in terms of facilitating wants, but more as being about controlling wants and behaviour. The conventional assumption is that children are born uncivilised, even wicked, and that their wants will inevitably be bad for themselves and for others, at least for a significant amount of the time, unless they are reigned in. Consent-based parenting, on the other hand, assumes that being 'self-centred' and doing the moral thing, co-exist. The goal of parenting is not to control, but to facilitate the child in self-maximising and following their intrinsic motivation. This goal relies on the assumptions that children are rational, creative, trustworthy and autonomous human beings living in environments where they have sufficient information to be able to make good decisions for themselves by their own lights.

Self-interest is, in fact, the only way to guarantee that those activities engaged in and decisions made are the right ones for any particular individual's learning, growth and well being. If children rely on parental perceptions of what is right for them, there is actually no way of guaranteeing that the individual child's unique self will be best served. This is because the parents are likely to be working on a preconceived agenda of what is best for children in general or from their own perceptions of the child, which, whilst they might be good approximations, can never be equal to the child's self-knowledge. Children whose intrinsic motivations are being followed and whose self-interest is being helped and facilitated will experience a greater satisfaction from life, a greater belief in their own ability to control their lives and an increase in well being and self-motivation.

Self-interest is also the optimal way for children to expend their personal resources, as they will do so only so long as they experience benefits. No matter how well a parent knows a child and no matter how well meaning we are as parents, we can never get inside our children's minds. Parents acting out of what they perceive to be a child's best interests will expend resources less optimally, either giving too much or too little in any particular area. Parents do much better to stay within the role of trusted advisor; offering information, best theories and criticism without presuming that in the final analysis they can know best for another person.

Parents are often concerned that if they concede that their children should act out of self-interest, they will be encouraging their children to become monsters who act immorally and with no regard for other people. Acting out of self-interest is often feared as being tantamount to acting badly - a license for abusive behaviour. This is neither what is meant by the theory nor what is experienced in practice. Doing the most optimal thing for one's own self-interest includes doing the right thing. Where it appears to someone that this is not the case, then it is reason and not coercion that is our best tool in convincing the protagonist otherwise. We cannot, ultimately, force someone to lead a moral life, but we can rationally convince children that a moral life and a self-interested life are mutually inclusive because the argument will stand up for itself. Immoral acts tend towards not only harming others, but also to being self-destruction on some level. It is arguable that harming others is not in anyone's self-interest because it involves giving up one's rights to expect respect and serious treatment in return.

By the same token, acts of generosity and service can be acts of self-interest without any contradiction. An aid worker in a famine may give up the prospect of home comforts and put herself into a situation of danger from a desire to effect change and live an altruistic life. Unless she is living her life based on notions of self-destructive irrationality, she will experience job satisfactions that are in line with her own self-interest.

Parents have no good reason to fear self-interest or to juxtapose it against morality. Within a family, of course, there will be a collection of self-interested individuals. It is often assumed that one person following their self-interest will inevitably lead to others having to surrender their self-interest. It is a common, but false, characterisation of TCS that it will be the parents who are the losers in non-coercive households. This is not the case! In chapter five, we will explore some reasons why maximising self-interest is quite compatible with finding common preferences in which everyone wins.

Coercion damages children. Theorising about our children and then acting on these theories, even when we believe that we are acting in their best interests, puts serious limits around their learning and growth. Our children's knowledge and well-being grows not from force or extrinsic motivation, but from the use of reason, the facilitation of intrinsic motivation and the encouragement of self-interest.

Part 2: Putting the theory into practice

Taking Children Seriously gives the theoretical framework for non-coercive consensual relationships between parents and children. There is not just one way to put this theory into practice. Solutions are as diverse as the families seeking them and as unlimited as the creativity available. Creativity is not the elite preserve of a few people or an attribute only of especially clever families. Creativity is what characterises us as human. Arthur C. Clarke illustrates this point in his now-classic novel *2001, A Space Odyssey*, with the constant refrain that begins as the ape, Moon-Watcher, evolves into a man,

> *"... he was not quite sure what to do next. But he would think of something."*
> (Clarke Arthur C., *(1973), 2001, A Space Odyssey,*
> p.37, London:Arrow Books)

TCS theory holds that there is always a solution. We may not know what to do next, but we can always think of something. We may get things wrong, but we can think again. We can afford to be optimistic. In the remaining chapters I want to explore what some of that optimism might look like.

Chapter four

Making the shift

In this chapter I will explore the practicalities of making the transition from conventional theories of parenting and education to non-coercion. I will briefly examine the differences between conventional parenting philosophies and consent-based parenting, focussing on the differences that constitute the paradigm shift to TCS. I will then move on to consider the importance of avoiding self-sacrifice, learning from mistakes (including the role of trust and apology), building a 'win-win' mentality, and learning to question everything.

A few fortunate people discover TCS before or very soon after becoming parents, and set out on this adventure from the outset. Most of us discover TCS some way down the line, often after consuming endless parenting manuals and experimenting with every form of conventional parenting. TCS demands a radical paradigm shift whether we have previously been liberal practitioners of attachment parenting or advocates of strict discipline. The process of entering that paradigm and making the changes to family life can be a daunting period. How to begin? How do we make this radical switch? These are recurrent questions. Part of the answer is being able to see just how different TCS is from any other theory of parenting and education.

Discerning the difference from conventional parenting

Those who come to TCS from a relatively liberal perspective often assume that they are simply moving slightly further down an already radical spectrum of parenting. This is not the case. *Taking Children Seriously* demands a major paradigm shift from any previously held parenting theories. Realising this is an important first step. Unfortunately, we seem to find the idea of moving along a spectrum a much more comfortable notion; however, it is worth being thoroughly convinced that only a major shift in perception will do.

From authority to fallibilism

Conventional parenting exists on a spectrum from strongly disciplinarian to liberal to laissez-faire parenting. Wherever conventional parents locate themselves along that spectrum, there is always a concept of authority and control at work. This is most obvious with disciplinarian approaches to parenting. Within such philosophies, 'love' and the 'best interests' of the child are often cited as the motivating factors in applying discipline, including corporal discipline. Thus Revd. Carl Haak maintains,

"Discipline is the order of God's government."

He follows this with the claim that,

"The rod and reproof are proper means of discipline."

In this case, the justification is an ideological religious one,

"Those children, to whom we give our affection and whom we love so dearly, are sinners, worthy of everlasting hell from the moment they are conceived."
(from www.rsglh.org.parental.discipline.html)

Haak is part of a large tradition of parenting, perhaps best epitomised by Dr. James Dobson, whose book *Dare to Discipline* continues to sell in its thousands. This tradition fears that, without strong correction, their children will be not simply spoilt, but damned. It is an argument from the child's best interests of the highest magnitude and with large stakes. The parent is the authority figure next in line only to God.

Such appeals to authority, however, are not reserved only for those who see themselves as delivering a religious duty to compel obedience. Those who want to take a 'common sense' approach still ultimately appeal to parental authority. There may be family meetings to decide on rules, but it is always the parents who set the parameters and who enforce 'appropriate consequences' when there is an infringement of the 'contracts' agreed to on the basis of parentally controlled choices. Thus one common sense advocate advises,

"Present some choices, and ask for his opinions; even if ultimately you make the decision, he will feel that you respect his ideas."
(www.parenting.org)

For those who do not locate authority in a punitive notion of God, but who want to appeal to more than the common sense authority of parents as bearers of wisdom and experience, 'nature' becomes a useful tool.

> *"The best known and most widely quoted guru of this approach is Jean Liedloff, author of 'The Continuum Concept.'*
>
> *"Working with the continuum concept, children are responded to, but should never be the centre of attention ... In this life apprenticeship Liedloff observes that very young children soon develop a strong sense of adult expectation and are obedient, quiet or even silent in adult company, conforming totally to the prevailing culture ...*
>
> *"Being allowed to develop naturally can sound so like being free to develop autonomously, but the two are not the same. Natural development is actually strictly controlled according to a preordained agenda of what it means to be 'natural', whereas autonomy has no agenda."*
>
> (*Doing It Their Way*, pp.30-31)

Within this style, trust and empathy are encouraged; guidance and example replace heavy discipline. Misbehaviour is redirected by means of natural and logical consequences and setting of expectations, (see, for example, www.attachmentparenting.org). It all sounds very reasonable, but it retains what every other conventional parenting theory has: an external authority, this time in the guise of nature itself. Almost all conventional parenting styles involve following some extrinsic authority, with the possible exception being laissez-faire or permissive parenting which contains other conventional errors. Only consent-based parenting inherently rejects the appeal to unquestioned authority, whether it is a particular religious characterisation of authority, the so-called 'common sense' authority of adults over children, or the authority of nature. The notion that we speak authoritatively by virtue of being parents, even parents who wish to appeal to God or nature, is inimical to the thorough acceptance of our own fallibility. We have to let go of any such opinion before we can make the required paradigm shift. We cannot take children seriously if we are ultimately going to appeal to some extrinsic authority.

Hearing what children say is not enough

Merely listening to children, whether to take account of their views or to negotiate compromises, is a feature of much conventional parenting theory, (particularly a tenet of liberal parenting), that can be hard to let go of. Listening and negotiating are very good things. They provide key elements in reaching common preferences, but they are not, of themselves, substitutes for common preferences. This is where a paradigm shift is needed.

Parenting theories that rely heavily on psychological theory are particularly intent on listening and hearing. The followers of Adler, for example, posit that misbehaviour results from children seeking attention, power, or revenge, or assuming disability. Parents are advised to 'listen' to their own emotional responses to discern the causes of misbehaviour. If they are feeling annoyed, it is likely that attention is being sought. They must either ignore this or deal with it through setting up special periods of attention. If they are feeling angry, a power struggle is indicated. They must take control and define their child's limited range of choices. If they feel hurt, it is likely that their child is seeking revenge and they need to rebuild the friendship. If they feel frustrated, then their child is assuming some disability and needs encouragement and self-esteem. (See www.lifematters.com/parentn.html).

There is at least, within this highly questionable psychobabble, a willingness to see 'misbehaviour' as a mistake rather than intent to harm. There remains, however, the enormous error of second-guessing a child's motives by dubious and emotive means in order basically to redirect and correct behaviour from an adult agenda of 'appropriateness'. Being 'heard' (even if this guessing method works!), is no substitute for having a solution that the child actually wants. The goal of TCS is that everyone, children and adults alike, should be genuinely happy with the agreed solution; whereas merely listening to a child, whether through adult emotions or the child's own words or emotions, does not promise any such solution. Common sense and democratic forms of parenting certainly take children into consideration. They allow that sometimes the child will win. They will also tend to suggest that life is a matter of constant compromise and that learning to give way graciously is both character building and a useful life skill.   Many people certainly do go through life believing that they are trapped, that they cannot achieve what they want or ever fully pursue their own happiness. Many people do go through life with fixed theories that they feel chronically unable to change. Many people go through life obviously believing that what they want is of secondary importance. Do we really want our children to be amongst those people?

Winning, without harming others, is possible. Reaching mutual common preferences rather than being heard but overruled by second-best compromises is attainable in families. Self-sacrifice is not the basis of a life well lived, nor is it the essential pre-requisite of a generous character. Listening to our children and hearing their emotions without finding solutions which they actually prefer, or inviting our children to negotiate within closed frameworks of already pre-ordained choices, are not enough to foster the rationality, creativity, autonomy and moral family relationships which TCS aspires to.

The myth of best interests

All parenting has the child's best interests at heart, unless, of course, it is deliberately abusive. Another key to making the shift to TCS is in ceasing to maintain that best interests can be in any way extrinsically defined. That is not to say that the parent does not have an enormous role in giving advice, best theories and information, as we have already explored; but, in the final analysis, best interest must be an intrinsic question of autonomy. No conventional parenting theory allows for this kind of integrity of autonomy. This is the case even for permissive and laissez-faire parenting which, by abdicating the parental role of trusted advisor, coerces children with a lack of genuine information from which to make the best choices. It is not for the parent to decide that it is in the child's best interest to receive the so-called discipline of God, or to follow what everyone agrees on as 'common sense', or to live a life without sugar, plastic toys, or TV, as so-called 'nature' intended. These are decisions for the child. The parent may have theories about religion or received wisdom or sweets that should be shared as fully as the child desires; but imposition of those theories, even those theories that the parent is quite convinced are correct and true, is not an option. Why not? Firstly, because no matter how convinced the parent is, they could still be wrong. Secondly, because no matter how well a parent knows their child, and no matter how much they love their child, they are not their child.

Love is not an excuse

A child is a separate person with a moral right to his or her own autonomy. Love is not a good enough excuse for acting immorally and deliberately to compromise that autonomy. The idea of loving coercion is pernicious, and runs through every strand of conventional parenting. Laissez-faire and permissive parents inflict coercive neglect in the name of love. Religious fundamentalists and other authoritarian parents inflict discipline, from spanking to time out to loss of privileges, in the name of love. Liberal parents seek to impose firm but loving limits. TCS completely eschews the idea that coercion of any kind, no matter how subtly conceived and implemented, can be an act of love.

Of course conventional parents, by and large, do love their children. TCS parents do not have the monopoly on love any more than they do on infallibility. The point is simply that a big shift in perception is needed for TCS parenting to take place; a shift away from the dogma that love justifies our coercion, of whatever form.

With no outcomes in mind

Another switch that characterises the paradigm shift between conventional and TCS parenting is the movement away from predicting or prescribing outcomes for our children. Authoritarian parents tend to have very clear pictures of the kinds of people they want and expect their children to become. The ideal is likely to include attributes like godliness, respect for authority, selflessness, industriousness, etc. Laissez-faire parents, on the other hand, may have hopes for revolutionary free-thinkers and independence. Those between these extremes, particularly those following democratic liberal styles of parenting, may have more amorphous aims in mind. Deborah Critzer, for example proposes that a childhood of *"respect, nurture and loving guidance"* will result in *"rounded, responsible, successful adults"* (see www.positiveparenting.com). TCS does not make any such predictions or encourage any kind of searching for outcomes in our children.

The conventional assumption is that children are products, and a product, as we all know, has to meet certain standards and criteria before it can be acceptable. For conventional parenting, this often means that children who do not meet the required specification are labelled. The labelling might be judgmental and intended to shame: 'Harry is a naughty child'; 'Becky is such a wilful, stubborn little girl'; 'Katie is a selfish little so and so'. Alternatively, it might be the kind of labelling which categorises children according to the growing plethora of 'syndromes'. Labelling neatly accounts for their faultiness without ever needing to question whether they are simply distressed human beings who are not resilient to all the coercion in their lives.

Imagine a busy school classroom. In an ethos where the product mentality is operating, a child who waits until everyone has got started on the work the group has been instructed to do before asking, *"And what should I do?"* attracts a host of 'faulty product' labels. Options are worked through. Is the child 'deaf'? Should the child be seen as 'deliberately annoying' and brought up to specification with behavioural management strategies? Should the child be seen as 'slow'? Should the child be given a useful label such as 'Asperger's Syndrome' or 'Attention Deficit Hyperativity Disorder', so that support, behavioural modification, and medication can all be brought to bear?

The product mentality of conventional parenting allows parents to long for their particular definition of a child masterpiece and encourages them to feel disappointed or even deliberately thwarted when this is not what they get. Most parents will agree that their child is unique. Yet conventional parenting also assists parents in attaching labels to their children that diminish the humanity of children who dare to display their individuality.

A clear example of this is the burgeoning number of children who are labelled with Asperger's Syndrome. The world is full of children (and adults), who talk before others have finished their turns, who introduce non-sequiturs into conversation, or who use language very literally. Many children have apparently quirky fears. Not everyone responds to social signals and eye gestures. Not everyone likes to be hugged. There are hosts of people who can amaze us with memories all the way back to babyhood, but still forget the last thing anyone said to them. Many people never conquer spelling and handwriting, but still soak up factual knowledge or become totally engrossed in specific topics to the exclusion of all else. It is not rare to find able people who seem to have great co-ordination in an activity like playing the violin, but none-the-less wander around with untied shoelaces, seeming clumsy, awkward and ill at ease in their bodies. Now there is a way of lumping all these observations together under one parent-absolving label: Asperger's Syndrome. It is, like all such labels, given with the best of intentions by those who want to help these 'different' children to fit in and be better products for their own good.

But why should a person be expected to be a certain kind of product in the first place? Is a tendency to become engrossed in particular subjects to the exclusion of other things objectively a bad thing? Or is it merely that it does not fit with the school regime of dividing the day up into artificial subjects, corralled into time allotments and controlled by bells? Is a propensity to express extreme and seemingly bizarre anxieties a symptom of a recognisable disease, or simply a child's response to various coercive stresses? Is Asperger's a pathology comparable to spinal paralysis or is it merely a convenient fiction - one which gives conventional parenting and education the justification for coercing highly individual children into conformity and narrow functionality?

If we lived in a society that truly tolerated difference and idiosyncrasy in all its human glory, then we would not feel a surge of relief on hearing our child being given a label that might at least mean some recognition of his difference. If we lived in a society that took for granted the premise that all education should be centered in the individual and intrinsically motivated by the learner, then the pursuit of 'special assistance' for children who are currently labelled would have no meaning. We do not live in such a society, of course, but that is not a sufficient reason to succumb to poor thinking. The way in which certain children are labelled is simply an extreme example of how the product mentality is used as a means of control and humiliation under the guise of 'for the child's own good'.

Simply thinking about our children in this demeaning way distorts the relationship and tends to exacerbate a whole range of subtle coercion. What we see of another person is only what is visible at that time. It is a small snapshot of a process, not a static definition. If our children are not products, then what does it matter that at any one moment a child is consumed with a particular subject, that at another moment a child interrupts a conversation, and that at another moment a child flinches away from touch? In a school environment it matters, because an artificial environment with a determination to inflict *certain* homogeneity of learning and behaviour is strongly in operation. This environment can be totally dispensed with in a home education setting, where only the child's intrinsic motivation and autonomy govern what is learned. This does not mean that an autonomously educating parent would never communicate information about what others might expect in given situations, but this can be shared as suggestions and opinions with no compulsion on the child to comply, and no judgements that define and objectify the child.

In a lifetime, we are lucky if we come to understand ourselves well. Even if we do achieve this, we never really know the whole. It is, therefore, presumptuous and demeaning to think that we can know another. We make observations, always partial, though sometimes helpful. There is nothing wrong with offering up observations that might help our children - "*If you don't look at people when you're talking, you might find that they think you're lying." "If you don't tie your shoe laces or ask someone to help you with them, you might have an accident on your bike."* This is reasonable and helpful; but it is not reasonable, helpful, or necessary to coerce a child into making eye contact by placing him in some behavioural modification programme or by constantly barraging him with information that he has long since tired of hearing.

The point is to help the individual child live his own life by his own lights in the way that most pleases him, not to mould him into a new set of attributes which seem more functional and pleasing to parents who want a higher level of product satisfaction. This is true, even when the moulding is dressed up in the insidious cloak of being for the child's 'own good'.

Once we have rid ourselves of the product mentality, the question of how we can help our children become more functional and acceptable, more socially in-tune, and more rounded individuals becomes not only irrelevant, but also meaningless. The only question that remains is, *"How can I help my child do the things he wants with his life?"* Children need to be free from being seen as products or from being objectified and defined by a list of subjective observations. They need parents who are unquestioningly on their side, not to impose their own or so-called expert agendas on their children in the name of loving assistance, but simply to assist their children in carrying forward their own intrinsically motivated lives in process.

The myth of natural consequences

Similarly, the paradigm shift that occurs in moving from any form of conventional parenting to TCS parenting necessitates letting go of notions of natural or logical consequences. Conventional parenting tends to elevate certain bad things happening to the status of being 'natural' or 'logical', by which is meant 'inevitable'. This is done in order to manipulate children's behaviour without parents ever having to take responsibility for this gross manipulation. 'If you don't eat up your breakfast, you will suffer from hunger'; 'If you climb in that tree, you will fall and hurt yourself'; 'If you run around the house, you will cause an accident'; 'If you don't go to sleep at a reasonable hour, you will make yourself ill', and so on. The parent makes it look as though the bad thing that is going to happen simply has to happen, but this is just not true. There are lots of different things that might happen if you avoid breakfast, like having a snack later, or finding that you are the sort of person who does not particularly miss this meal. Hunger will result only if the child is refused any food two hours later. This is not a natural consequence, but a parentally decided-upon consequence meant to teach the child a lesson. It is nothing more than a cruel and coercive deceit to say, 'I told you so', **and** claim that the consequence is nothing to do with the parent.

There are times when bad things happen despite our best efforts to prevent them, but TCS parents can go a long way to minimise such times. They can give lots of information about nutrition and body clocks and individual patterns of eating and how to get access to food at lots of different times. They can discuss the safest ways of climbing and the best kind of trees to use and find out about other climbing opportunities to extend these skills. They can ensure that children can sleep when it suits them and do not have to be artificially and coercively either woken or forced to sleep.

The cry often comes back from conventional parents, 'But how will he ever learn about...?'. The simple answer is that children will learn through information and discussion. Children do not have to experience artificial consequences dressed up as 'natural' in order to learn the laws of physics or how their bodies work or what people's attitudes to different sorts of behaviour might be. Children are not going to learn how to think rationally and creatively about problems and how to overcome them by being fed a diet of lies about what will happen to them if they try out certain things. If there is a good reason why a child should not do something, then the reason should be able to stand for itself and not need the back-up of made-up 'consequences'. If the reason not to do something does not stand up to scrutiny, it should be revised, not propped up by coercion in the garb of 'nature' or 'common sense'.

Summarising the paradigm shift

The shift from conventional to TCS parenting is an enormous leap of perception and lifestyle. It demands that we give up any allegiance to extrinsic authority in favour of recognition of our own fallibility. It requires that not only do we listen to and hear our children, but that we actively work with them to find mutually delighting solutions. It requires that whilst we give advice as parents, we desist from insisting that we know what is best for another autonomous human being. It does not allow us to cite love as a motive for coercion, or to prescribe the product our child should be. It is a paradigm shift that exposes the myth of natural consequences and places us in a completely new environment for parenting. Once we have made this paradigm shift, our lives will never be the same again. We will find ourselves facing new challenges in parenting, some of which will be particularly acute in the early stages of making the shift. It is some of these early challenges that I will examine in the remainder of this chapter.

Avoiding self-sacrifice

So, you have made the paradigm shift and are eager to start parenting in a new and consensual way. The aim is to build consent via common preferences, but for parents who are new to this way of thinking it often seems much easier to fall into self-sacrifice. We desperately want to stop coercing, but we are not used to the kind of creative problem-solving that achieves common preferences. In an attempt to avoid coercion at all costs, we short circuit the entire creative problem-solving process and just give in. Of course, it does not really help. Few of us can sustain self-sacrifice without building up stores of resentment that are likely to erupt in coercion at some point, either in a massive blow out or in a steady, corrosive stream of coercive remarks or subtle manipulations. Furthermore, we are denying our children access to the very creativity and rationality that is at the core of TCS and which makes it so much more than merely non-coercive parenting.

When all our rationality and creativity fails - as it sometimes will, given our fallibility - it is better for a parent to self-sacrifice than to coerce. This is an extreme default, however, used in failure and as little as possible. It is not a recommendation or a normal way of relating to our children. That said, self-sacrifice happens because we are fallible. It is likely to happen more frequently when we are just making the transition to a new paradigm and have few models of common preferences to draw on. Most parenting theories, after all, have some concept of how noble it is to sacrifice ourselves for our children, so it is an easy mode to slip into. So, how do we know when we are self-sacrificing and what can we do about it?

We know that we are in a state of chronic self-sacrifice when we never actually prefer the outcome of any given problem-solving attempt. We know that we are stuck in this dead-end arena when we begin to think that it is inevitable that parents should feel this way. If we are telling ourselves that we must lose in order for our children to win, then we are definitely self-sacrificing. It is likely that this will make the whole situation volatile, guilt ridden, and liable to an ugly melt-down at some stage. Parents who continually self-sacrifice are not giving their children any example of problem solving and getting the best from life in the long term. Rather, they are presenting a skewed picture of childhood as the time for satisfaction, before the child grows up in the real world of becoming a long-suffering doormat. This does our children a tremendous disservice. It deprives them of a lifelong model of positive and consensual problem solving. It gives them so little to look forward to, they can hardly be blamed if they become grasping and uncaring while they have the limited chance as children. Whilst the children of self-sacrificing parents become ever more insistent and demanding that their needs and wants are met this minute without question, the parents themselves are likely to become more and more depressed and resentful and ever less creative.

We can only begin to break this cycle when we convince ourselves that life does not have to be like this. If we believe that self-sacrifice is not noble but actually draining and harmful, then we are more likely to resist it. If we are convinced that there are solutions out there, even when we fail to find them, then we are more likely to start again positively. If we are convinced that each scenario does not require that some lose whilst others win, that we can in fact build consent into our family relationships, then we will not be satisfied with self-sacrifice. Instead, we will reserve self-sacrifice only as that infrequent moral default when all else fails us.

Consent is optimum when everyone in the family, adults and children alike, take themselves seriously, and each expects to live the life that they truly prefer within the family group. When this is happening, adults and children can all be open to changing their preferences without ever fearing that it will mean doing something they really do not want to do. This releases an enormous flood of creativity for solving problems consensually. To stop self-sacrificing, we need to think seriously about what it is that we want. This does not mean that we have to become intransigent or unable to revise our theories. We should start from what we want, not from what we do not want. We should believe that we could get what we want, and communicate to our children that we can get what we want without in any way needing to coerce them. Children who are used to self-sacrificing parents may be sceptical about this, but they will soon come to trust the process if they see that everyone can win, and that their parent's new found seriousness about their own needs is not going to be at the children's expense. In the longer term, children will be very happy to have a creative model for finding common preferences, which they know will serve them in continuing to get what they want as they move into adulthood. The future will look as flexible and full of possibility as the present.

Building the win-win mentality

The key to avoiding self-sacrifice is in building a win-win mentality. This is something that conventional parenting does not prepare us for. Few of us believe that everyone can win. We are schooled to accept that only some can win, that we must compromise, that we have to take turns at getting what we want. TCS proposes that we think like this because we fail to use our resources of creativity and rationality. If we determine to work together to find common preferences, it can be done; the more we do it, the more creative we get and the more new knowledge we generate.

Being able to do this rests on the separation of two important theories. The first is that we are fallible. Since we are fallible, we will make mistakes and we will sometimes fail to find solutions. At any given time, we can work only with the knowledge and theories that we have at that moment. These may sometimes be inadequate to the situation, resulting in a dead end, self-sacrifice, or even coercion.

The second is that there is always, in theory, a solution. We may fail to find solutions because of our fallibility and limited knowledge at any one moment, but this is not the same as believing that no solution was even theoretically possible. There was a solution, probably several solutions, but we simply did not find it on this occasion. The self-sacrificing or coercive parent may be willing to acknowledge some level of fallibility (though children are usually characterised as **more** fallible than adults), but they are generally unwilling to admit that a solution could have existed in theory. Rather, they insist that their actions were inevitable, that someone had to lose. TCS proposes a very different fundamental premise, namely that solutions always exist, at least in theory, whether or not we manage to find them in any given situation. TCS parents believe that this premise is yet to be falsified, and in practice it gives them an essential basis for building the win-win mentality.

Let us consider the Jones family, which has three children aged 18, 14 & 12. Mum Jones has heard about TCS and thinks it might be for them, but has lots of questions. Dad Jones thinks it is mad. Sally (18) thinks it is OK for older teenagers, but surely the younger ones **need** coercion to keep them in line. Joanne and Peter think it sounds great, but they are sceptical too - they still think Mum will coerce them when the chips are down.

Today is a busy day. Dad has a pile of work he wants to get through. Sally is leaving for an important holiday with friends and wants a lift to the airport. Joanne really wants to see a certain friend today, who lives some distance away from the city so there is no public transport. Sally and Joanne have already had a row. Sally thinks Joanne's trip is unimportant as she could go any time and Mum should take Sally to the airport instead of Joanne to the friend's house. Joanne thinks Sally always gets everything her way - she has not seen her friend in ages and there is a bus straight to the airport. Peter wants to go to a park today, as he has been practising some new stunts on his skateboard and wants to do some more. He also wants pizza for lunch. Mum wants to get through the day sane, and hopes for a cup of coffee (with caffeine!) at some point. Dad says it is nothing to do with him, he has to earn a living and, by the way, 'I told you you couldn't all get what you want.'

Of course, the best scenarios are going to occur when everyone in the family subscribes to TCS, but even here there are possible solutions. We have to remember that solutions ultimately have to be the ones that particular people prefer. Knowing that a solution is theoretically possible does not always give us the creativity to find it, but it does make us look at things differently. It is an enormous mind-shift that has a real effect. We also have to remember that the final solution may not look anything like the initial problem/s. The art of finding common preferences is the art of creativity and openess. We can change our preferences; something better can come along at any moment.

Any number of things could happen. Dad might be persuaded to take just a long enough break to take Sally to the airport, freeing up Mum to drive with Joanne and Peter to Jo's friend's, pick up the friend, and take them all to a pizza restaurant near a park. The girls could have time together and Peter could skateboard. Mum could get two cappuccinos at the restaurant and read half a novel in the park.

Dad might be totally intransigent and remain outside of the loop. Mum, having talked some more to the children, might realise that there is a new movie opening today that Jo and Peter both want to see. She could drop them at the cinema on the way to the airport. Before setting out, she could ring the mother of Jo's friend, who might agree to bring her daughter for an overnight stay later that day. Then, after the friend arrives, Mum and Peter could head for the park via McDonalds (Peter having changed that preference), and Mum could relax in the park café with delicious real coffee and cakes.

Dad may remain fixed, but Mum finds that Jo and Peter would rather go bowling than go to a friend's or to the park, so she drops them on the way to taking Sally to the airport and joins them there later for her coffee.

Alternatively, Dad stops being a grump and realises that he has a client he could visit who lives close by Jo's friend. He could take her and still be working and he'd prefer that to the office. Mum will take Sally to the airport, then have an afternoon to herself in the city. Peter is happy to stay home - with Dad out of the office, he can have access to the computer without interruption. Or something else entirely different could happen ...

The point is that there is not some fixed, pre-determined solution out there that has to be mystically divined, nor that there are no solutions and someone has to suffer. Rather, the point is that we can build consensual 'win-win' families if we start by believing that solutions are always theoretically possible. Solutions are as practical and available as our own creativity. What prevents us finding solutions is not that they cannot exist, but simply that we are fallible.

Learning from mistakes

Owning and recognising our fallibility does not mean that we have to get stuck on it. We make mistakes. These mistakes should not lead us to despair, but rather, should be used as opportunities for learning and growth. Conventional wisdom tells us that mistakes are bad and that guilt will follow. Conventional parenting seems to have two main responses to parental mistakes. The first is to wallow in guilt, feeling that we can never get it right, endlessly agonising and mentally beating ourselves up for not being able to do it all, be it all, and self-sacrifice with a smile. The second is to claim that we can only do what we can do, that we can only be 'good enough'. This must inevitably mean that sometimes our children are going to have to lose and get used to the fact that this is what the 'real world' is like.

TCS takes neither of these coercive paths. We make mistakes, but we recognize that agonising and living in guilt just undermines our motivation and traps us in a futile cycle of negativity. We can act only from what we know in the moment, but this neither necessitates nor justifies coercion and immorality. TCS parents own their responsibility towards their children and do not diminish this with weak arguments about inevitability when they fail. At the same time, TCS parents see no need for these failings to be a reason for paroxysms of guilt. We should always apologise to our children when we make mistakes. We should always be able to recognise our responsibility and not merely justify our errors. This done, however, TCS parents can then rejoice that they have seen the error and can now criticise it, learn from it and move on.

As long as we are alive, we should always be learning. What better way to learn than by a constant process of conjecture, refutation and new knowledge? Being able to say that we were wrong and then move on to develop a new theory are matters for celebration, not guilt. Certainly, there are things we will and should regret; but being able to think about these things clearly, and to work out how to change without being burdened by self-loathing is much more likely to effect change that will benefit both parent and children.

Sometimes we do not understand why we make particular mistakes. We may have all sorts of triggers that are hidden deep within our psyche or which arise from ideas that we have imbibed without ever being able to articulate them. We may never fully get to the bottom of such inexplicit theories, but we can learn to notice our triggers. We can spend time thinking about ways to disengage or behave differently when those triggers arise. Our actions are not predetermined. We always have a choice. Knowing this can make it much easier to avoid or recover from even the most ingrained of mistakes.

When we have come to see our mistaken behaviour as something that we can change and use as a springboard for learning, we also start to treat our children's mistakes differently. Children are fallible, too. Conventional parenting often assumes that children do certain things to test their parents, or deliberately to engage in a power struggle over rightful parental boundaries. TCS rejects this kind of thinking, which sets children up as the enemy. Mistakes occur when we lack information or creativity. Children, like adults, have limited knowledge. Mistakes are bound to arise. There is no need to regard these mistakes as a deliberate challenge or the setting out of battle lines.

Let us take Max. It is a sunny Sunday afternoon and Mum and Dad are settled with their novels in garden chairs. Max is playing in the garden. There is a sudden noise of breaking glass. Mum and Dad look up to see a large conservatory window shattered. Why did Max do such a thing? It might be that Max did not understand about trajectories and just kicked his ball at the wrong angle. It might be that Max desperately wanted to explore the properties of glass and no one would help him so he conducted an experiment by himself without good information. It might be that Max had been trying to get someone to play a ball game with him for the last four Sundays, but was constantly told to go away. In his desperation, he had tried this out to get some much-needed attention. Max made a mistake. He is not evil. Perhaps his experiment has gone wrong, or he has acted from insufficient knowledge, or he has operated with a faulty theory. This does not make him an out-of-control monster who is begging for clear boundaries. He is a human being who needs some different sorts of information and input.

Question everything

In the final analysis, we make the paradigm shift to TCS most successfully when we are able to question absolutely everything. Why should we all go to sleep at 11p.m. and get up at 7.30 a.m.? Why should parents (or anyone), be seen as figures of authority? Why do we so easily believe that acting immorally towards our children (in the form of coercion), can be justified for some perceived benefit like clean teeth? Why should not our children stay in their pyjamas all day? Why do we think the world will end if our children drink coke or love watching TV? The list is endless. When we start to take our children and ourselves seriously, then real individuals with real preferences and real problems to be solved replace all the received conventional wisdom about how we should think and behave. It is a process in which our whole worldview is likely to be constantly changing. It is both enormously scary and endlessly liberating.

TCS is not simply a slightly more radical form of liberal parenting on a spectrum that we can choose to slide back and forth along. TCS parenting demands a whole paradigm shift to a world of consensual relationships where everything, absolutely everything, can be and will be questioned. In this new paradigm, parents, accustomed as we are to fixed solutions, often desperately reach for practical examples of how to live with autonomous children. There can be no definitive answers, but it is possible to explore scenarios and begin to get a feel for a new and consensual way of working. It is to such scenarios that we will turn in the next chapter.

Chapter five

Everyone's a winner

In this chapter, I will focus on building consensual family relationships and explore how to find common preferences. In particular, this requires relationships in which there are no opposing sides. It necessitates learning to seek solutions outside the immediate situation, pooling creativity and fostering an environment in which all parties are open to changing their first preferences. I will seek to show how self-interest and common preferences are mutually inclusive, and consider the uselessness of the notion of 'fairness' as it is commonly conceived. I will look at the voluntary nature of parenthood and how parents give up certain rights in order to take on the responsibilities of parenting, arguing that this is a freely chosen benefit and not a sentence for a life of self-sacrifice. In examining these themes I will use some hypothetical examples of situations to demonstrate what consent-based parenting might look like.

On the same side

Conventional parenting polarises families. On one side there are parents, struggling to retain control and impose boundaries that are deemed to be in their children's best interests. There is an assumption that, at some level, children and parents are working towards opposite ends, and it is up to the parents to take the reigns and steer the family to the good. This is the case even when the steering comes in the form of sugar-coated 'loving guidance'. On the other side there are children, constantly testing the boundaries and needing to be taught lessons. Without 'loving discipline', the wisdom runs, they will become selfish, insatiable monsters. The notion of artificial boundaries, which we will explore more fully in chapter six, is at the core of this polarised thinking. It is also aided by the myth that we cannot all win, that there must be compromises and losers. We need to reject these assumptions. In TCS families everyone is expected to be on their own side. Each individual knows best what he or she wants and prefers. Far from creating untold conflict, this allows for rational discussion of how all of these interests can be met through common preferences where everyone wins. There is no such thing as doing something in the 'family's best interest' when one or more members of the family are deeply unhappy with the solution.

Being able to create an environment in which everyone wins relies on several things. It is absolutely necessary that children can trust that they can enter into the process of finding a common preference without fear of coercion. It is only when they can do this that they will be able to see that they can change their preferences and still get what they want. Without this trust, they are much more likely to stick rigidly to their first preference, fearing that if they show any open-mindedness on a particular subject they will merely be trampled upon. Similarly, parents must be willing to go into the process without having already decided what the outcome must be. They must be willing not simply to desist from coercion, but also to use all their creativity to find common preferences.

So, parents and children are not working against one another, but are working for consent and **common** preference. What might that look like? Let us imagine the Potter family. The Potters have five children under the age of seven: Jenny (7), Sam (5), Lucy (4), Katie & Rachel (both 2) and baby Ben (3 months). Mum is exhausted. She cannot remember what a preference is, never mind find one. Dad is supportive of mum and TCS, but also exhausted – he is the only earner and things are pushed at work. Ordinary things are starting to get Mum down. The laundry seems to conspire against her. She longs to have a tidy corner of the house, but cannot ever seem to catch up. There are constant running squabbles that never seem to be resolved between the children.

Firstly, it is worth noting that this just is a difficult situation, and introducing coercion would not change that. Screaming does not get laundry done and making one another miserable is not going to help anyone. Mum clearly needs help. Could Dad change his work schedule to make things more flexible? Are there good friends or grandparents or babysitters or other adults who could help? Adding adults or friendly teenagers to this situation could improve things enormously, even if it is only very part-time assistance.

It might be that Jenny, Sam and Lucy (at least), have friends they could go to spend days or parts of days with. Conversely, it might be that the children could invite friends to spend days or parts of days with them in return - they may be a lot happier and play with more contentment when there are **more** children that they especially want to be with. Increasing the number of children, although it might not seem like the best solution, could actually help enormously.

Turning to a different part of the problem, a complete decluttering of the house and re-arrangement of all the storage could make quite an improvement. Mum probably feels too exhausted to do this alone three months after giving birth, but she could hire someone to do this and a thorough clean - a one off payment to set up more helpful ways for the future. Or she may have friends or family who would be prepared to give this kind of help. Perhaps a local teenager would do parts of the cleaning for reasonable rates, or perhaps the teenager would play with some or all of the children for certain periods in return for computer access. On the laundry front, Mum could go to a charity shop (or several), and buy lots of clothes for the children so that she would need to do only one mammoth laundry session once a week, or this could become a regular and manageable contribution from Dad.

Mum could change her preferences about how tidy the house really needs to be and feel more comfortable in a different environment, or she could think about what are the things that make her most comfortable and just concentrate on those. This might mean reaching a common preference about having a tidy bedroom or a tidy zone around a special chair.

Mum should also enlist the support of the children - 'I want us all to get what we want so I need your ideas all the time and we need to work together to find the things that work best for us'. Tiredness and mistakes are travelling companions, so Mum needs to be ready to see her mistakes and apologise. It also helps if, when the children make mistakes, she can see them as just that; failures of creativity by people who lack practice at trial and error solutions, but who are trying to get better. Mum should not start seeing the children as monsters conspiring to make her miserable. What would be more helpful, would be thinking ahead and planning to have lots of favourite activities available for stressful times. A pile of books for reading to the twins by the favourite chair for feeding the baby; a good selection of videos easily accessible; favourite CDRoms pre-installed and easy to start; a table with art things out all the time might be life savers in those moments when there seems to be lots of demands all at once. Another useful idea is to have lots of food and drinks accessible in forms that the children can get for themselves or with the minimum of help.

With so many small children, it will be a good idea to build in extra time for making trips or meeting appointments. Stressful rushes to get ready can easily sour otherwise enjoyable events. Mum may also think of ways to build in escape plans from unwanted events or activities that the family soon feels they want to get out of. On other days, some creative thinking might be required to meet different wants.

Take a day when everyone except Sam wants to go to a local meeting for home educating families. Is there a friend Sam could spend the day with? Perhaps Jenny and Lucy could go to the home educators' meeting with another family, and Mum could go to the park with the others. That way, Jenny and Lucy get to see their friends, Sam is pleased, the twins are just as happy with the park and baby has an onboard milk supply. There might even be a really good café in the park that Mum loves! Or perhaps everyone would really prefer to go out to a fun fair and buy ice cream. Or the solution might be something else entirely different…

The 'Disney' solution

The important thing is that a solution is found which everyone generally prefers. There are many ways of problem solving, as many as our joint creativity allows. Sometimes a useful way to problem-solve is to take apart the expressed preferences and see what are the elements that are making something a 'want'. One night, for example, the Lewis family decides they would like to eat a take away. John is a vegetarian and wants pizza. Liz says she would like tandoori chicken and the parents both decide on different curries.

The youngest family member, Ben, is at a friend's house, but will be home to eat. The parents decide to get him some roast chicken and chips, as this is a regular favourite. The food is bought and everyone eats, (except Ben, who will be home later and whose food is kept warm). When Ben arrives home he is upset that his parents have bought chicken and he says he wants a 'whole pizza' like John.

At first the parents are stuck. Dad and Mum have had alcohol with their meal so do not want drive back to the take-away stores. Dad is worried about the waste and thinks that Ben should just eat the chicken and tries to convince him that he will enjoy it. Mum agrees that they should have phoned and actually asked Ben what he wanted. She is sorry, and she is happy to eat the chicken cold next day for her lunch, but she cannot think how they are going to get the pizza as the store will not deliver such a small order. Then Mum notices what Ben is actually saying, 'I want a whole pizza in a box like John.' So Mum says, 'We've got some frozen pizzas in the house, lovely big ones with the topping you like. How about if we cooked one and used John's box to serve it in?' 'Yes,' agrees Ben, 'I'd like that pizza, if I can have John's box.'

We have to be prepared to do a bit of creative deconstructing of preferences; to ask, what is actually wanted here? Sometimes, it is not as obvious as we think. Taking things apart can lead to a good solution. Of course, sometimes that does not happen, and then we may need to try another method of problem solving.

On the *Taking Children Seriously* internet discussion list, one of these methods of problem solving has become fondly known as 'the Disney solution'. Jane wants to go ice-skating, Philip wants to go to the movies, Ellie wants to go to the park. No one seems to be open-minded. Mum says, 'How about a trip to 'Disneyland' instead?' Suddenly, everyone is in agreement. It does not have to be Disneyland! The point is, most families have a few activities that they really enjoy and which might break an impasse. It might be that the solution needed is something that is not amongst any of the initial preferences, but something entirely different; something that does not have the feel of one person being talked into doing another person's choice but, instead, enables everyone to think outside of the current box.

Creativity and changing preferences

If children trust that they will not be risking coercion by taking part in problem solving, if their creativity is valued and used, then the idea of changing preferences becomes much less threatening. Parents can generally see that the ability of children to change their preferences is a crucial one, but it is much easier to overlook the necessity for adults to change their preferences too. In chapter one I looked at how coercion damages our ability to think and at how we can develop entrenched theories. This can happen to anyone, at any age, but adults have generally encountered much more coercion damage and are particularly likely to have areas that they find it virtually impossible to discuss rationally and openly. I will examine some of these areas in more depth in Chapter Six, but it is worth noting at this stage that parents must be willing to change their preferences, if they are to facilitate consent as the *modus operandi* of their families.

Changing our preferences is not the same as self-sacrifice. If we are looking for genuine consent and common preferences, the changes in our thinking have to be real. If we feel that we are merely compromising, or if we feel resentful or uneasy about solutions, then there is no point in kidding ourselves that we have arrived at a common preference. Changing preferences is not easy, especially in entrenched areas, but the more we commit ourselves to finding consensual solutions and the more we practice finding common preferences, the more it will happen.

One thing that we can do to help the process is to ask ourselves if the thing we are expressing a preference about is really an area where we have the right to interfere. I might prefer a tidy house, but does that give me a right to insist that my children should have tidy bedrooms any more than I would have the right to insist that an adult friend should have a tidy house? I might prefer a vegetarian diet, but does that give me the right to impose a vegetarian diet on my children?

I am not suggesting that these (or any others), are simple, clear-cut areas. The examples above are complicated by the fact that we have a special relationship with our children, and they might be happy to reach a common preference with us even if we do not have a 'right' to expect this. The examples are also complicated by the practicalities of sharing a home, and by the fact that we have a responsibility as parents to share information and our best theories about hygiene and life-style and diet and anything else. Even with these provisos, however, it can sometimes help us to see things differently if we simply ask ourselves, 'Would I presume to interfere so closely with an adult friend? Is this properly an area where I should be expressing a preference?'

Another way in which we can help ourselves to change preferences is to seek both criticism of our theories and new information. All too often, we live within a milieu in which consensual living is viewed as anything from impossible, to dangerous, to quirky. Within such a milieu, it is hard to find a wider pool of creativity and criticism to challenge our more coercive or entrenched theories. To some extent, we have to be prepared to do this for ourselves, but there is help available. Children are often willing to act as astute critics. If they trust that it is safe to do so, they will generally be very generous with their criticism, pointing out coercion and presenting cogent reasons why our pet theories might be wrong after all. More widely, there are other people trying to live consensually, and gaining access to their ideas and criticisms can be an invaluable aid in working on entrenched theories. It might be through the regular *Taking Children Seriously* journal, or the more immediate medium of the TCS Internet mailing list, or through building relationships with particular families.

A third way of helping ourselves to change preferences is to ask ourselves what we care about most. Are we really more wedded to an idea that watching more than two hours of TV is bad for a person than we are to our child's happiness? Do we really think that avoiding a glass of cola is more important to our child's well being and thinking than avoiding massive distress? *Taking Children Seriously* is not a burdensome code to be slavishly followed and implemented, but a positive choice about how we value one another and want to behave morally and creatively towards one another. Simply reminding ourselves of this can often help us to begin solving problems that seem to have come to an impasse. At other times, we may simply need more time. A theory may be so entrenched that we are not ready to examine it at all. We will need more practice at finding common preferences in easier areas before we are willing to return and expose this difficult ground. At such times, the best thing we can do is to back off. There are plenty of other problems to be solved.

Self-interest and common preferences

In chapter three, I proposed that self-interest is a good and proper thing for a child to exhibit. I now submit that consent-based family relationships are desirable and possible, and that the goal is to find common preferences. Are these things really compatible? Why should a child who can have what she wants be interested in helping other family members to get what they want? Is not the best we can hope for a compromise that people can live with? Is not the self-interested child going to take up an intransigent stance and repeat his position or demands until they are met, in the full knowledge that he is not going to be coerced?

It is important to stress that common preferences are not compromises. If there is a compromise, then it is likely that someone is feeling coerced and someone's self interest has been disregarded. If a child appears intransigent, then perhaps he is unconvinced that it is safe to let go of his original preference and explore new ideas that might bring him something that he prefers more. Alternatively, he may have already reached a good solution and the criticisms of it are genuinely unconvincing to him. A common preference is reached only when every one of the participants genuinely prefers the solution. If every one genuinely prefers something, there is no conflict with self-interest. Children are interested in helping the whole family, parents and siblings, to reach such common preferences. They trust that, in the process, they will be fully respected and may very well find something that they prefer over their original suggestion. If a child knows that she will not be coerced, there is no reason to cling to a demand without the possibility of thinking or problem solving. After all, it is quite possible that her first suggestion will end up being preferable to everyone.

The myth of fairness

One thing that often stands in the way of finding common preferences is the myth of 'fairness'. Conventional parenting tells us that all children should be treated the same or equally. If we buy Lizzie a bar of chocolate we should get an identical bar for Tim. If we spend an hour reading to Tim, we should spend the next hour drawing with Lizzie. Most of us were brought up in families where parents and grandparents told us, 'You can't give to one without giving to the other'. Surely, it is common sense that we should treat our children fairly and equally, that we should not discriminate between them? This is not taking children seriously. Children are individuals. If we buy Tim chocolate simply because we bought some for Lizzie, we are not taking any notice of Tim's individuality and real preferences, relating to him by means of a mechanical principle.

The notion of fairness promotes a climate of sibling rivalry in which children are constantly watching one another and their parents for signals of unfairness or favour. Conversely, if we treat each child as an autonomous individual with his or her own preferences which we want to help them achieve, then both fairness and rivalry become superfluous. Lizzie wants chocolate and a movie. Tim wants to spend some time reading with mum and would like pizza for tea. Perhaps all of those things are simply achievable. Perhaps there is some problem. The answer is not to tell Tim, 'Well, today we are all going to the movies. I'll buy you some sweets and I'm sure you'll enjoy it, really. I read to you yesterday. So it's only fair'. The answer is to find a common preference. That may mean that everyone will do the same thing because everyone decides that they had not considered the idea of going bowling and they would all prefer that to their original ideas. It may mean Lizzie will end up going for a bike ride with her friend and stopping off at the sweet shop on her way, whilst Mum and Tim snuggle up with the book and later Dad cooks paella, which everyone prefers to pizza. When we take each child seriously, we have to abandon any allegiance to mechanical rules.

The voluntary parent

If you think that finding common preferences sounds like a lot of hard work, try asking yourself which form of parenting offers you an easy life. We are sadly mistaken if we become parents thinking that there is an easy option. Relationships take work. Important relationships can take lots of work. TCS offers not only the prospect of relating to our children in the most moral way, but also offers a real process for consent, in which parents as well as children get what they want. TCS is a parenting style that entails constantly creating new knowledge; that is hard work and sometimes difficult to implement, but as Sue Cvach has expressed,

"The satisfaction of parenting with morality and consent always means that optimism is in the forefront."

As parents, surely a good measure of what we want is in terms of promoting our children's happiness and facilitating their growth by their own lights? Parenthood carries responsibilities, but there is no need to see those responsibilities as terrible burdens or, most insidiously, as sacrifices. If I buy myself a delicious box of chocolates or a sweater that I really love or a novel that I have been longing to read, I do not think of the money used to purchase the item as being sacrificed. I certainly weigh up whether this is what I want to do with my money at that time, but, having made the decision, I do not resent what I am giving up to get the longed-for item. The giving up is voluntary, a simple way of getting something that I prefer and can enjoy more than the money in my purse. Children are not commodities, of course, and the analogy is limited; but, for parents, giving up certain aspects of a life without responsibility is not a sacrifice, but a change to a new and preferred state.

We should enter into parenting with an intention to promote our children's autonomy, delighted when we can help them get what they want from life, and thrilled that we can facilitate their growth, learning and happiness by their own lights. This is not a burden or a sacrifice, but a parental preference. When we can start thinking and feeling like this, parenting ceases to be the chore that many conventional parenting theories would have us believe that it is. It is a sad reflection on our notions of parenting (and perhaps on our concept of relationships in general), that we conflate something which takes a lot of creativity, risk, learning, and openness to change and challenge, with being something sacrificial, burdensome, and an occasion for resentment.

The two do not have to go hand in hand. An athlete who sets her heart on running a race in a particular time has to devote a lot of energy, commitment and creativity to achieving her goal. She does so willingly. She is happy to alter her diet radically and to devote her time to realising her desire. Her goal is challenging and difficult, but it still remains voluntary - her most important preference and a joy to execute.

When we are able to see our relationships with our children like this, and not as onerous and tiresome, then we will not grudge the creativity and time that we put into finding common preferences. Rather, we will be exercising our own preference to relate to and help someone we chose to bring into the world. Finding mutually preferred solutions is not galling, but delightful. Changing our view of the process in this way is vital if we are serious about parenting in a way that enables us to relate morally to our children.

 TCS goes to the core of the relationship. The parent, as well as the child, is taken seriously. This means that the parent will need to find ways to change not just their outward behaviour towards their children, (an extraordinarily difficult thing to sustain even if it is sometimes the fallible default of failures of creativity), but also how they think and feel about their children. Merely changing the outward behaviour towards our children might be a stepping stone or a default, but the real paradigm shift to taking children seriously comes when our inner thoughts and feelings change.

This is, admittedly, no easy feat when we have become sadly accustomed to thinking of morality as being merely about our external treatment of others. Not only, however, is it an enormously liberating aim to pursue, but it is only a change in inner conviction that ultimately makes taking children seriously authentic. Our

children know when our responses are faked or forced. We also
know ourselves that we can only 'make' ourselves change our
outward behaviour for a limited period, as Sue Cvach put it,

> *"Especially when the whole house of cards comes falling down
> when the effort to keep up the appearance of change is too
> much and a meltdown or some such occurs."*

It is the inner change of paradigm shift that allows us as parents to
stop treating our relationship with our children as an exacting
demand that has been imposed on us extrinsically and instead to
start creatively enjoying it as a source of learning, growth and freely
chosen preference.

Finding common preferences

So, you want to help your children to find common preferences, but
you are as fallible as the next person and come with your own raft
of entrenched theories, one of which is likely to be the pervasive
idea that most of the time someone has to be disappointed. There
are no rules for finding common preferences. What works for one
family may be of little use to another. Believing that a solution is
possible, even if we do not find it, is a major part of the process.
Also, it is important that the participants believe themselves to be
on the same side, rather than seeing themselves as adversaries.
They must be are able to discuss their preferences openly, teasing
out the vital elements of a preference that may lead to new
solutions, and being able to risk changing preferences without fear
of coercion. Creativity and self-interest are fully valued and utilised.
Moreover, the process of finding common preferences flourishes
when concepts such as fairness are abandoned, and when parents
are able to acknowledge that parenting is a voluntary role and not
an enforced burden. We begin to find common preferences when
we live without boundaries, as I will explore in the next chapter.

Chapter six

Without boundaries

Conventional parenting relies on boundaries. Whether their adherents claim that the boundaries come from God, common sense, logic or nature, they are put forward as fixed, irrefutable points. Despite this, no two parenting theories will ever totally agree on what these boundaries are. There are areas that people perceive as resistant to non-coercion, some of which are commonly cited as areas where responsible parents should impose boundaries.

We commonly think that rules will keep us safe, but they will not. Rules are mechanical, contrived and extrinsic. When a situation arises in which the rule does not apply sufficiently, or where an exception is needed, or when the extrinsic control is removed and the child is alone to make a decision, rules are often inadequate. Rules cannot substitute for our ability to think and solve problems. We are at our most creative and innovative best - not to mention safest - when we are assessing every aspect of a problem or situation in order to arrive at a solution that is uniquely tailored and appropriate.

Boundaries limit thinking. Life without boundaries demands constant and creative thought. Boundaries place extrinsic controls on us. Life without boundaries promotes intrinsic motivation and the constant growth of knowledge that accompanies it. Boundaries are artificial. Life without boundaries is about constantly pushing the limits of knowledge and what is possible. Boundaries give us rules to follow in model situations. Life without boundaries gives us the autonomy, flexibility and rationality to negotiate real situations, even when the models fail to apply.

In the film, *The Matrix*, the central character, Neo, discovers that he has been living in a world that is constructed for him, inside a sham of reality that is designed to maximise extrinsic control. Moreover, he discovers that he can choose not to accept this version of reality, but instead seek the truth. In a final telephone call to the former masters of the Matrix, the illusion of reality, he says,

> *"... you're afraid of change. I don't know the future. I didn't come here to tell you how this is going to end. I came here to tell you how it's going to begin. ... I'm going to show them ... a world without rules or controls, without borders or boundaries, a world where anything is possible. Where we go from there is a choice I leave to you."*
>
> (*The Matrix*, closing scene)

This choice is not merely a fictional one suitable for a futuristic film script. We can choose to live without boundaries, but we will probably start off feeling afraid and wanting to know, at least, how to begin, especially in areas where it has previously seemed to be self-evident to us that coercion has to be a necessary feature of parenting.

The age of reason

The notion that children can be given incremental freedom as they get older and become 'more reasonable' is a pervasive one. In particular, babies and toddlers are targeted as the main focus of boundary parenting. There is a widespread resistance to the idea that this age group can live without coercion. In practice, *Taking Children Seriously* begins at many ages, depending on the growth of individual families. For those, however, who are fortunate to discover it before they become parents or very early on in their children's lives, there is no reason why consent-based living needs to be withheld from babies and toddlers.

The needs of young babies may be intense, but, in general, they are fairly simple in range. Food, warmth and physical closeness tend to feature high on the list. Despite the lack of verbal articulacy, most parents quickly become adept at interpreting the signals of what is liked and disliked. To mangle a quote from the Monty Python sketch, *The Last Supper*, the baby *"... may not know much about language, but he knows what he likes"*. This is what TCS means when it credits babies with rationality. The theory is not that babies are born arguing the validity (or not), of Hegel's dialectic, but rather that they are born with the ability constantly to create new knowledge and follow their intrinsic self-motivation and self-interest. As such, babies are rational and we can find common preferences with them. The same is true as babies grow into toddlers. We may be able to use only very simple words or we may need to rely on visual or practical demonstration, but we can definitely discern toddlers' preferences, and clearly see that toddlers are able to move to new preferences or (in their own way), suggest new solutions to adults. Rationality does not require that children first reach a golden age of reason. It simply relies on not interfering with children's ability to express preferences and not preventing them from reaching new and mutual preferences.

Let us take Joe, a nine-month-old who comes across a bottle of bleach and starts trying to unscrew the lid. The laissez-faire neglectful solution is to leave him to it. 'He'll soon learn not to mess with bleach!' The coercive strategy is to take the bleach away from Joe, probably with a firm 'no', perhaps with an attempt at distraction if Joe is in a liberal household. The common-sense rationale is that the bleach could do Joe harm and that coercion is a lesser harm (if it harms at all), than the risks of swallowing bleach.

For Joe, something else is happening. His needs and desires are not being taken seriously. He begins to learn that, whilst his parents say they love him, they will still do mean things to him (by his lights). Already, Joe is being given mixed messages about the correlation of love and hurt.

TCS suggests not that we glibly let our children fend for themselves, but that we work with the child to find something the child would prefer to play with or drink or shake or smell. It might be that Joe is simply after a drink. It might be that Joe would like a bottle of some harmless liquid that he can screw, unscrew, pour and sniff. It might be that this particular bottle is attractive and feels good to hold. Could the bleach be emptied into another container, the bottle scoured and another liquid put in to retain the feel? It might be that Joe would prefer an ice cream or a trip to the park or a big bowl of finger-paint mixture to anything that the bottle could offer. The point is that it is highly unlikely that nine-month-old Joe was trying to commit suicide with the bleach. It is possible for an adult on his side to work with him to find what he wanted to get out of the exploration, and to enable him to achieve it or move on to another better exploration.

Or, let us take two-year-old Adam. Adam's mum thinks that a daily bath is an integral part of any two-year-old's daily routine. Today Adam disagrees and is quickly becoming upset. Adam may not be able to articulate very clearly why he does not want to have a bath, but that need not stop a TCS parent from working with him to find a solution. Does Adam really have to have a bath at the same time every day? Why? Perhaps Adam would like Mum or Dad to be in the bath with him or he may need a change of bath toys or some soaps that can be painted on the tiles. Perhaps Adam would prefer a shower instead or a trip to the swimming baths or a paddling pool in the garden? There is nothing to be gained by forcing a child to take a bath in the name of loving boundaries, but a great deal to be gained by working with Adam to find a common preference.

Safety first

From sharp tools to fires, to staying out alone, there are assumptions about externally imposed safety rules shared by conventional parenting and education. I want to argue that these actually compromise safety by impeding the growth of intrinsically motivated decisions about personal safety. Moreover, the rules impede the growth of knowledge, hedging possible learning around with artificial boundaries.

Imagine two seven-year-old friends, Sadie and Lucy. They are enjoying splashing in a bath on a hot summer's evening, when their attention is caught by a high-up bathroom cabinet. They use a chair to reach the cabinet and begin to explore. Inside they find a large bottle of pills - pink pills that look like sugar-coated sweets. They manage to open the bottle and pour out the delicious looking, though potentially lethal, pills.

Lucy suggests they try some. Sadie says they should ask an adult what they are. She says that she knows that things kept in these kinds of bottles tend to be medicines, not sweets, and medicines can make you ill. Lucy replies that this is silly. She insists that medicines make you better, not ill, and adds that if she asks her mum she will just be shouted at and maybe smacked, because she is not really allowed to touch anything in the cupboard.

Sadie agrees that medicines can make you better, but says that her mum has told her that each medicine is meant for certain kinds of illness and can hurt you if you do not have the illness. She also says that her mum has told her that some medicines can hurt you even if you only take a little bit and that smaller bodies can get more hurt. She says that her mum has told her that some medicines are not so strong and might just give you tummy ache or not do anything bad if you tried a bit. She points out that she and Lucy do not know what sort this one is, so they really should ask someone to help them. Lucy says angrily that adults do not help children, they just tell them what to do. She adds that she knows her mum will just punish her for breaking the rule about the bathroom cabinet and she wants to find out for herself. Sadie replies that her mum does help her and she does not want to eat any tablets without knowing more about them.

In this scenario it is the child who has been brought up with rules who is much more in danger. Lucy's information about medicine is much sketchier than Sadie's because her rule-bound parents have seen no need to provide her with the truth that medicines vary in strength and effect. They have replaced information with the simplistic rule of 'don't touch'. Lucy's desire to engage in illicit behaviour is also increased by the rule-bound mentality. She sees her parents as the opposition to be thwarted and hopes to be able to get away with something without their knowledge. This attitude makes no sense to Sadie, who, living in a TCS home, sees her parents as trusted advisors who will only say, 'well, two of these pills could make you feel quite ill and eight could kill you', if that is really the truth. Sadie knows that if she were at home, not only would her parents offer good information about these particular pink pills, but would also help the girls play with empty bottles or buy sweets so that they could play at pharmacies safely. Sadie knows that her parents would help her to make her own good decision and would not treat her as though she was an irrational or suicidal imbecile. Lucy knows no such thing and the chance of being able to indulge in the forbidden over-rides her rationality and her friend's refutations.

The conventional parent might object that the solution is for Lucy's parents to become more coercive. After all, they could have put the pills in an even more secure location. This is true, and whilst it may be a good idea to store dangerous drugs carefully, 'child-proofing' of itself is never a complete safety precaution; whereas having a child who will seek advice before ingesting a bottle of medicine is extremely safe. The conventional parent might insist that another thing that is extremely safe is to ensure that you have a child who just will not break the rules. They might argue that Lucy's parents had obviously not been strict enough and the rule had not been sufficiently impressed upon her. This is a dangerous argument. Some children, sadly, have wills that break easily; their creativity and drive to find their own solutions is soon crushed with even small amounts of coercion. Many children, however, are more resilient, and the force needed to impose external boundaries can quickly spiral, making the home a virtual war zone.

Two-year-old James, for example, has been told not to touch the electric sockets. His parents begin by saying 'no' and trying to distract him each time he approaches a socket. James continues to be interested, so the parents say 'no' more sternly and remove James to his bedroom for a few minutes each time he approaches a socket. James is undeterred, so his parents add a light slap to James' hand on each occasion, but still to no avail. Now James' parents reluctantly, but for his own good, decide to spank him each time he tries to touch a socket. James is very distressed by this development, but does not give up. Where can these conventional parents go next? Life in this household has become a long round of conflict. The electric sockets will be just one of many battles being fought.

The TCS parents will first examine their theories about electric sockets. Are they a danger to James? In most homes with modern wiring, the insulation is such that a child poking in a finger will come to absolutely no harm. If the socket is a real danger, perhaps this is the problem that the parents should really be addressing. In the meantime, they need to find ways to communicate the danger to James, ways to find a common preference around his safety that does not rely on lies or artificial rules that just beg to be broken.

Let us return to Lucy and Sadie. Lucy is out of hospital after the tablet taking incident. Her parents will not let Sadie come to their house to play anymore, convinced as they are that their daughter would never have broken the rules and nearly died if she had not been playing with 'that girl from the house with no rules'. Lucy's parents have used the whole incident to impress on their daughter that she must always follow the rules. 'If you break the rules, you could die', has become a favourite saying. Lucy is playing outside with a group of children and Sadie joins the group. The neighbourhood is reasonably quiet and traffic-free and the pavements quite wide. The children are enjoying a game of 'tag'. There is a sudden screech of tyres and a car rounds the corner. The teenage driver, who is being pursued by a police car, loses control of the vehicle and it mounts the curb. Children scream and run. Sadie jumps into the road, leaving the now dangerous pavement for the safety of an area she assesses to be clear. Lucy knows that on no account is she to step off a pavement without an adult. She knows that breaking the rules not only gets her into trouble, but also is dangerous. She freezes in the path of the oncoming vehicle.

Even if we succeed in making our children live by extrinsic rules;

even if we can make them accept rules without having to resort to beatings; even if we choose our rules carefully and impose only a few rules that will tend to hold in most cases; even then, our children will not be as safe as children who are given honest information about risks, children who know that they can get all the help they need in negotiating risks, children who are accustomed to finding the best solution for any particular situation.

We cannot foresee every situation. Life is risky, and there will always be tragedies whatever parenting method we use. I contend that the children most likely to be safe are those who can think most rationally, who can access advise without fear of coercion or lies and who have no motivation to do something just because it is forbidden. TCS children will certainly take risks, but they will take them rationally, advisedly, and with the best preparation to get the learning they want without exposure to unnecessary and unwanted danger. Ultimately, the only safety that any individual has is that which comes from intrinsic motivation. Assisting our children in developing this safety does them an enormous service. Coercing them to accept extrinsic safety rules leaves them exposed and vulnerable to irrational decisions. Moreover, such coercion impedes the growth of knowledge.

Five-year-old Darren loves to play with fire, but how he learns about it will depend on what kind of home he grows up in. Let us imagine Darren in a conventional household. The rule is that Darren must not play with fire. Fire is dangerous. He could hurt himself or even burn down the whole house and kill the whole family. Two things could happen. The first is that Darren will find a way secretly to break the rule. In this case, he will either satisfy himself that his parents are talking lies and nonsense and are not to be trusted, or he will have an accident of some nature, perhaps minor, perhaps more serious, but certainly avoidable if someone had helped him. The second is that Darren will obey the rule and cease all exploration in this area. In the short term this may look fine to the casual observer, but in fact Darren is left with irrational and untrue theories about fire that he will eventually pass on, and his own growth of knowledge in this area will have been cut off. Darren cannot learn about fire and combustibility and the properties of materials and all the lines of inquiry that might arise from such experimentation. In a laissez-faire household, by contrast, Darren could pursue his experimentation and learning, but would be more likely to do so dangerously, not having access to good advice and assistance.

Darren's life would be completely different in a TCS household. His parents would give him good safety information about fire, outlining the possible dangers, but without exaggeration or pressure. They would explore the kinds of experiments Darren would like to do and discuss the best ways to go about them. They would assess together which experiments he could do alone, which would require help, what safety devices would be good to have on hand and where the best place would be to conduct the experiments. Darren could develop good theories about fire, pursue his own intrinsic learning and stay safe.

Life and risks are intrinsically bound together. Sometimes we choose risks quite rationally in order to learn something or enjoy some particular experience. This said, there are many dangers that are avoidable. The safest course is to parent our children so that they will trust our advice, critically assess our best theories and make their own rational decisions.

Bodily autonomy

Diet, exercise, personal hygiene, health and sleep are all areas that present themselves to conventional parents as areas where control is needed. These are areas in which we constantly revise and develop our theories; yet, all too often, we expect our children to develop good theories whilst being coerced. There are two issues here for TCS parents to consider. The first is whether, as parents, we have any right at all to so much as pass comment on such personal matters. The second is whether our actual theories, if we do have a right to share them, are correct.

Do we have the right to pass comment on what are essentially matters of bodily autonomy? If we were asked that question in relation to another adult, the likely answer would be 'no'. We recognise that people have the right to eat what they like, bathe when they like, keep fit in their own way (or not), and sleep when it suits them. Even if we are able to see that children deserve the same rights to bodily autonomy as adults, however, we might object that when we are living in close proximity with others, we do not expect them to assert their rights all the time. We might, for example, feel that is not unreasonable to expect a certain level of personal hygiene from a husband or wife, or we might reasonably request a partner to wear a particular style of clothing for an important company dinner party. In the same way, we share space with our children. Although we have no *right* as such to dictate what they eat, when they shower, whether they should use deodorant and how much sleep they need, it can be quite reasonable to share our theories about these areas. As Sarah Lawrence notes in *TCS Opinion*,

> *"When people are sufficiently committed to one another to share their lives ... seeking common preferences can and ought to replace standing on one's rights..."*
> (*TCS Opinion*, TCS Journal, no.27, p.4)

This does not mean that children should automatically accept their parents' theories. It is a recognition that in close relationships there is an arena for comment and sharing, provided it does not become coercive hectoring and provided that the parent is willing to desist if no common preference is found.

Mandy is a teenager who is experimenting with her looks and dress. Some of her choices seem rather daring to her parents, but they are keen to respect her autonomy. Mandy is also interested in religious beliefs and practices. She tells her parents that she wants to spend some time visiting different places of worship, finding out more about different beliefs and what they might mean for her. Her parents advise her that her favourite short red skirt is likely to be seen negatively at both the local Church and the Mosque, a few streets away. They tell her that she may not be taken seriously, and may even meet hostility. They suggest that more conventional clothing might help if she wants to be able to talk to people without eliciting negative judgements. Mandy decides that this is good advice and follows it.

A few weeks later her father tells her that some distant relatives are coming to stay. He says that they are rather conventional people who expect to be deferred to by young people. He asks that Mandy wear 'sensible' clothes while they are staying. Mandy thinks about this and decides that it is a bad idea. She tells her father that, in her own home, she feels that it is an unacceptable intrusion to dress according to the prejudices of virtual strangers whom she may very well never see again. She lets her father know that, while she was willing to make changes in order to visit other people in their own place of worship and to enable her to learn the most from her visits, she cannot see that this is a similar situation. She sympathises with the fact that her father will probably get adverse comments from these relatives, but she thinks that he is quite able to deal with this in his own home with people with whom he has no regular contact.

After some thought, her father agrees that Mandy is right. He can probably deflect any criticism with gentle humour and need not be so anxious about the visit.

While we do not have a right to tell our children what to eat or wear, it is reasonable for us to make suggestions and share opinions, though we need to remember that our theories might be wrong. When it comes to issues of bodily autonomy, food and sleep are the two areas that seem recurrently to cause the most concern. Food is an emotive area about which all sorts of claims and speculations abound. What is considered 'good for us' changes frequently on either scientific or quasi-scientific grounds. Even worse, there is a whole industry of dubious theories purporting to tell us that we should eat only what Stone Age people ate, or should follow recommended lists according to our blood group, or should eat only gluten on days of the week with a 'w' in them. Added to this, parents often aim to control what their children eat in the name of 'best interest'. Children are autonomous human beings, capable of making good decisions, given good information. We should certainly share our theories about food and nutrition and dental decay with our children, but we should not exaggerate, lie or claim to have found the final truth. Given our own fallibility and the shifting ground of this area of human knowledge, the likelihood of having the truth is very remote and our children may have very good criticisms to offer us.

The fear is that given free choice, children will gorge on an endless diet of cola, crisps and chocolate - but why should this happen? Certainly, children's intake of these items may rise from its former controlled or forbidden levels, especially when restraints are first lifted; but why should we assume that our children are so irrational that they will not be able to find a particular way of eating that works for them? We are not simply leaving them to it, after all, but are there with advice and suggestions.

Phoebe comes from a vegetarian home where sugar is restricted and there is a definite emphasis on 'good' foods and 'bad' foods. She is allowed limited amounts of 'good quality' sweets, carefully screened for additives, and has no meat products in her diet. Phoebe is not forced to eat or even try any foods, but nor is she allowed to try certain things. When Phoebe is three-years-old, her parents discover TCS and start to rethink their coercion around food. First, they relax about sweets. Much to their surprise, Phoebe does not eat mountains of sugar. Her intake of sweets rises, but she is not hyperactive or sickly or any of the things that her parents would have predicted just six months earlier. One day, at dinner with friends, Phoebe asks to try some ham. Her parents regress slightly and start to tell her about the horrors of meat production and how this was a living animal that was probably badly treated. Phoebe, now a confident TCS four-year-old, replies that she knows all these theories, but she thinks she might like ham. Her parents agree, reluctantly, and Phoebe loves the ham. Within six months, Phoebe's openness and criticisms of her parents' food theories have won her parents round, and they all eat meat happily. This is not to say that respect for autonomy is incompatible with vegetarianism. It is simply to illustrate that theories in this area, when all the studies have been weighed up, are ultimately very personal. A child is just as likely to make objectively good decisions as an adult. What is more, even when adults feel that children are making bad decisions, they cannot be sure that this is the case. If the parents are offering theories that are convincing on their own merits, there is every chance that the child will agree. Parents should be wary of damaging their children's mental well-being and sense of autonomy for the sake of a dietary theory that might be out of vogue in two years time.

Letting go of the control of our children's sleep patterns can be another major hurdle in living without boundaries. Henry is a three-year-old who likes to be awake at night. His parents see this as a problem, but can gradually come to see that it is possible to find a common preference with Henry. They might decide to take turns to stay awake with Henry. They might decide that the parent with a job to get up for early each morning should get some sleep and the other parent adapt their sleeping pattern to Henry's pattern. This parent might discover that the night-time is a great time to be awake. She might enjoy 24 hour shopping with Henry or find the quiet is conducive to writing the novel she always wanted to produce, while Henry watches favourite videos or plays nearby, knowing that his parent is available if he needs anything. They might find that Henry would gladly sleep earlier in the evening if some condition were changed, perhaps the lighting or noise levels or temperature or having someone with him while he is falling asleep. They might find that they can both sleep while Henry stays awake playing if he can play quietly in their bedroom or close by or watch a video in their room as they are falling asleep. They might find that the problem is not that Henry likes to be awake into the night, which they can accommodate with some creative thinking. Rather, the problem is that Henry is booked into day-care at 8.30

a.m. each morning and the late nights mean that he would prefer to sleep till about 9a.m. or sometimes later. Can the family take Henry along to day-care later? Can one or both of the parents alter working schedules? Does Henry want to be in day-care at all? If not, how is the family going to solve that problem?

By working creatively on a given set of evolving problems, common preferences can be found. Starting with set ideas about what time children of three should be in bed or how many hours sleep a three-year-old *must* have will not produce solutions, only battles which someone must lose. Individuals vary. Some of us need or would prefer ten-hour blocks of sleep. Some of us thrive on very little sleep or prefer several shorter periods of sleep. Some of us relish mornings and others the night. Why should children be denied the right to find the pattern that works for their particular body and mind at a particular stage of their life?

A common objection is that people have to learn to fit into 'the real world'. In fact, the real world, which we all live in, is becoming ever more flexible. School is not compulsory. Most appointments can be arranged at our convenience. Work patterns are increasingly complex and open to negotiation. Leisure, shopping and so much else is increasingly available 'out of hours' in supermarkets and high streets, as well as via the Internet and new technologies. Event-driven living is replacing the agrarian concept of rising and sleeping with the sun or the industrial concept of nine till five or shift workdays. Children who are able to grow up respecting their own preferences, and without the sleep disturbances so common to those of us who have grown up with coercion, will be best placed to take part in a flexible world with a sense of making their own choices.

Ultimately, we cannot control our children's bodies. Children who are repeatedly coerced around food are highly likely to become adults with food problems, possibly even serious eating disorders. Children who are forced to sleep or wake at times that do not work for them are likely to be tomorrow's insomniacs. Children whose bodily autonomy is not respected can hardly be blamed for having little self-respect or for taking dangerous and avoidable risks in attempts to gain some self-control, whether through anorexia, taking drugs without information or becoming irrationally averse to taking any exercise. As with safety, the best way to help our children make good decisions about nutrition, exercise, sleep, hygiene, hair length or any other issue of bodily autonomy, is not through coercion, but through rational conjecture and refutation.

Pulling together

Conventional parenting theory strongly suggests that children have to learn to lose, often a great deal of the time. Building win-win situations often appears elusive, even impossible, to parents who are used to such conventional thinking, but win-win solutions are possible, always in theory and, as we become accustomed to finding common preferences, increasingly in practice. Many conflicts seem to reach an impasse simply because we are so ready to set the supposed good of the family group against the preferences of the individual. We do well to remember that the good of the family group is not being served if in fact one of its members is suffering. The group's good becomes a possibility only when everyone within it prefers what is happening.

This myth usually presumes that whatever the parents deem to be important at any given moment is definitive of the family good. If the parents think it is teatime and everyone should sit down together and eat the same food, then this is characterised as the family good.

Yet many parents remain convinced that sometimes their children just have to bow to the needs of the family group. Tidying up, chores and sibling rivalry are areas in which this conventional wisdom operates most strongly. Fourteen-year-old Sophie lives with her mum (an artist), her dad (a therapist), and her two brothers Jake (eight) and Charlie (eleven). Her parents are trying to be non-coercive, but they have an entrenched theory that the family has a form of contract to one another and should each do their share as regards chores. Charlie has given up arguing and does the least possible to avoid conflict. Jake is adept at using his status as youngest to avoid coercion. Sophie has become the focus of conflict. Sophie hates being made to do set things at set times, though she will often spontaneously join in with polishing or vacuuming when she is not under pressure. Her parents take this as a sign of intransigence and irrationality, claiming that if she can see the need to help, she ought to be able to help when they feel it is most needed. Sophie has some good arguments. She points out that her mother's attic art studio is always messy, so surely her mother can see that tidiness is not essential always and everywhere; rather it is a matter of such things as function, taste and individual comfort level. Sophie points out that the reason for having a pristine hallway and stairs is that her father's clients come through that way to reach his therapy room. Not all children live in homes with this kind of dual use, and it is not her responsibility to provide a work environment for her father. She argues that she did not consent to being born and does not feel that she has actually had a choice about entering into any contract with her parents. Sophie says that she is quite happy with a certain level of mess. It is her mother and father who have the highest standards and comfort requirements, so they should find ways of getting their needs met that do not involve coercing her. Sophie also points out that the reason that they cannot ever find a solution, instead, going round and round in circles and unhappy compromises, is that they do not even have the same problem.

Her parents' problem is how to keep the house clean. Since they have a theory about a necessary level of tidiness they constantly look for any mess and focus on this. Sophie's (and Charlie's) problem is that they feel very unhappy when their parents clearly disapprove of them, but also feel unhappy when they are doing things against their will. The children have theories that parental approval and being able to do the things they want are important components in their lives and they are constantly looking for ways to maximise these. Unfortunately, the tidying the house saga compromises both areas. Sophie suggests that she would be happy to help her parents solve their problem and asks that they help her with her problem, too.

Having identified the problems, Sophie and her parents finally set about looking for solutions. Lots of suggestions are made. They could hire someone to come in and clean the house. Sophie's father says he does not like the idea of a stranger in his therapy room where he keeps confidential records. Sophie suggests a locked cabinet. Charlie says he does not think there are enough bins and laundry baskets in the house. Jake says his friends have a lot more machines in their kitchen, like a dishwasher and microwave. Mum says that she is constantly uneasy with strangers coming and going in the house and feels under pressure to please these strangers. She suggests that they dig out the plans they had for an extension to the side of the house so that the therapy practice would not intrude on their home and she would not feel so anxious about tidiness. This would also give space for Charlie and Jake to have their own rooms, which would solve other problems. Everyone talks about the household chores that they enjoy even occasionally. They agree that those things that no-one likes or which no-one would enjoy regularly should be the things they pay for help with.

If everyone were happy, the discussion might end there, with recognition that no one within the family should be put in a position where they feel either coerced or disapproved of. A new problem, however, might be thrown up by the solutions that have been offered. Charlie might ask how much these solutions are going to cost and wonder whether paying for all this will mean putting off the purchase of a computer he has been longing for. This might lead to prioritising the solutions or refining them or even to going back to the original problem and criticising the theory that the house ever needs to be as tidy as the parents first suggested. They will keep going until they have a genuine common preference because it is spurious to assert that the good of the group sometimes has to take precedence over the good and happiness of any one. The group is made up of the family members. If one of them is unhappy, then the good of the group is not being served, no matter how much it is pretended otherwise.

Manners and mores

Adults often expect and require a degree of respect from children that they do not feel the need to reciprocate. Many children are taught never to tell lies, whilst their parents routinely lie to them. 'We can't afford that chocolate bar'; 'You'll become ill if you watch too much television'; 'All your teeth will drop out if you don't brush them twice a day', and so on, are simply examples of a huge repertoire of stock responses that many parents use for convenience or control.

In the film *Liar, Liar* the father (Jim Carrey), explains to his son Max (Justin Cooper), that adults have to tell lies in order to get by in the world or to remain polite. Carrey explains that without 'white' lies, life would be untenable. In the scenes that follow, we see how difficult life can become when his character, a divorce lawyer, is compelled to be bluntly honest because of Max's birthday wish that his father cannot lie. Adults can plainly see that lying is not always a bad thing and is sometimes a very good thing; for example, few people would think that being truthful about the whereabouts of a Jewish family, if asked by a Nazi soldier, would be moral. Yet, despite this, we are much more simplistic in our expectations of children and honesty. Children who use lies for their own survival are easily labelled as sneaky and untrustworthy when they may in fact be acting in their own best interest or lying for some other moral reason.

Another required feature of children's 'manners' is that they should not interrupt adults. In adult conversations, there is a constant to and fro of interruption that is taken as part of normal banter and is acceptable in most circumstances, (exceptions might be when men dominate conversations to the exclusion of female colleagues or when interruptions become aggressive). When children are doing the interrupting, however, there are often accusations of rudeness and disrespect. What is actually occurring is the mobilisation of a pecking order. Children are at the bottom of a hierarchy. What they have to say is deemed to be of less value. If they intrude on an adult conversation, it must be for some reason that is trivial and easily dismissed. 'Go and play and don't bother me unless someone breaks a leg or there is blood,' may be said in joking tones, but it none the less reveals an attitude that children's concerns are intrinsically less worthy of attention than anything an adult could be saying. There may be times when an adult needs some privacy or a set period of time to achieve a task, and there is no reason why common preferences cannot be found to ensure such times. There may equally be times when children want uninterrupted private time. That said, there is no room in consensual relationships for simply presuming that there is a hierarchy in which children's concerns, needs and comments are discounted and ranked last. The appearance of conventional 'good' manners is not as important as taking our children seriously.

Children who always say 'please' and 'thank you' and who speak with deference towards adults complement the conventional dream of truthful, unobtrusive children. There is no intrinsic reason why children accustomed to being taken seriously and who live in households where consent is fundamental should be rude and aggressive, but neither is there any reason for such children to be artificially grateful or pleading. Such children are likely to be used to speaking as human persons of equal worth. There are times when a 'please' or 'thank you' is simply a small token of courtesy that might be used by adults and children alike without any coercive undertones. If it is required, however, that a child say please for everything he receives, from food to toys, from trips to attention, then something is wrong. Should slaves be grateful for emancipation? Should women be grateful for the vote and equal pay? Those groups might certainly appreciate these things in their lives and might admire those who helped them gain these rights, but they are basic human rights. Is a child any less human, even to the extent that he should be grateful if his parent feeds him or spends thirty seconds listening to him? Parents have a duty towards their children. Gratitude is not owed and cannot ultimately be compelled, even if children are forced to mouth it. That is not to say that relationships in which people feel thankful for one another cannot or should not develop, but such feelings are not to be coercively manufactured.

A question of resources

Another constant boundary issue relates to the use of limited resources. Parents frequently believe that they have little or no control over these limitations, and so their children, too, must simply accept them without question. This is particularly the case with budget constraints or limited time. We do not have to be rich to take our children seriously, but we do have to be creative. Taking children seriously is not a matter of providing everything that comes into our children's head on demand the instant they ask, but of creatively finding common preferences. This will certainly lead to very new ways of considering and using family budgets, but it does not lead to inevitable bankruptcy. Moreover, things actually acquired may look very different from any initial wish list.

Many times, conventional parents tell children that they cannot afford a particular wanted item when the truth is that it is simply not their priority. If children are to be taken seriously, there must be some basic honesty and openness about family finances. Is more being spent on fuel than necessary simply because parents have not researched alternative suppliers? Does the 'essential' food bill include regular adult 'take-aways' when the children are told that take away pizzas are an unaffordable extravagance? Do the children agree that expensive furniture and new clothes are vital, whilst extra televisions for family members are out of reach? Would the children rather use the money from piano classes for a year on a trip to Disney land or vice versa? The questions and answers will be endlessly various between different families. The point is simply that everything can be questioned. Sometimes the answers will be as surprising as they are creative.

Twelve-year-old twins, Toby and Daisy, would like to have more technology available. There is often too much competition for the family's one television and, under the previous coercive family regime, they were often expected to give way to their little brother, Jim (aged six). Toby would like more opportunities to explore the Internet and design web sites, but the one family computer is over-subscribed and his father's work seems to take precedence. Toby has watched the Discovery channel at a friend's house and would particularly like a television with a cable connection. Daisy loves movies and would like a video to go with a television in her own room. Jim adds that he would like to have the cable cartoon channel and a play station. The family sit down and talk about the wish list, at which point Mum adds that she would like the film channel and Dad says he would like a more modern computer with specifications more suited to his current work. The family is not rich and the wish list involves money. Dad suggests he could take on an extra freelance contract for a limited time or Mum could do some agency nursing (her former career). Jim says he does not like it when Mum is not there at bedtime. Toby points out that he was hoping for some time soon with Dad to help him with some programming. Daisy says she would be happy to contribute some recent birthday money from grandparents and Toby agrees that he would like to do this too. Toby suggests that they could clear the attic and do a boot-sale and could probably raise at least another £100 that way and have some fun doing it.

This prompts Dad to remember that he has been meaning to sell an old record collection for some time. Mum says that she and Dad had been discussing the two living room sofas. Both are rather worn and shabby and she had suggested taking out a loan to buy new ones. She now thinks that perhaps the sofas could hold up for another year or two and instead they could use a loan for a second computer. Toby suggests that some of the other items could be obtained second hand or reconditioned. Daisy suggests they make a priority list and that they should talk about how each of them might feel about allowing other family members to use items in their own rooms. Whether the family end up with all of the proposed items or none of them or something completely different is not the issue. There is no fixed outcome except that it should be mutually agreed. Whether the family budget is enormous or extremely modest, the key is creativity and not deciding beforehand that something *must* be done in a certain way or that something else is simply not worth considering.

Being creative with time is as important as being creative with money. All too often adults set up time constraints without sufficiently thinking through the implications for children or considering alternatives that might be required. Most families need at least one adult to work for a family income. Most families will, at some point, need to make appointments with doctors, lawyers, plumbers. Many families will schedule classes or driving lessons or plane flights. It is not that these things do not matter, but that they do not matter more than our children. They are areas in which we can reach common preferences. Can we rearrange work commitments, either in terms of time or venue, to fit in better with family preference? Can we build in flexibility with certain kinds of appointments? Can we arrange alternative care or activities for our children so that they are not committed to unnecessary journeys on our behalf?

Pam has an early morning doctor's appointment. She has made the appointment at a difficult time in that her five-year-old daughter, Ellen, likes to wake up slowly and enjoy a leisurely breakfast while watching a favourite cartoon. Pam's husband Steve can often start work at a flexible time, but has an important client to meet. The doctor Pam prefers to see works part-time and her appointments tend to get booked up well in advance. Pam is very concerned about a particular health issue and does not feel that it would be a good idea to wait much longer. The conventional answer would be to take Ellen along, whatever her protests, and to argue that her distress is nothing in comparison to her mother's current anxiety and needs. Some parents would even claim that if Ellen objects, it is she who is being coercive and not Pam. Coercion requires power. Children do not have power over their parents, whereas parents have an automatic power that is easily abused and widely supported. This one instance of coercion may do no damage to Ellen, but we cannot know that. It is immoral to take such a risk and highly disrespectful of Ellen's autonomy.

So what can Pam do? She could ask the elderly lady over the road, who loves spending time with Ellen, to come in and stay with her for an hour. She could explain to Steve that this appointment is very important to her, so important that it might be worth his considering changing his appointment with clients. She could reconsider whether one of the other practice doctors who are more available might not be just as sympathetic and helpful, and rearrange to mid-day when Ellen is happy to come along, or to evening when Steve is back home. She could talk to Ellen about making the trip to the doctor's a special and fun event. Perhaps Ellen could sleep in a comfy track-suit the night before and be tucked into the car with a blanket and warm drink for the journey. They could take a favourite snack and picture book to the waiting room, or borrow Steve's hand-held game boy or his portable cassette player with headphones and story tapes. They could go out for a special breakfast after the appointment or have a breakfast of popcorn at the nearby cinema while seeing a cartoon movie in which Ellen has expressed interest.

When we begin from a fixed point and fixed preferences, we are unlikely to succeed in living consensually. Instead, we will end up with coercion or self-sacrifice. When we are willing to let go of the myth of inevitable and immutable outcomes, we free up the creativity to find common preferences. It might be that the solution will contain one or more of the initial starting points. Pam might keep her appointment without any coercion, for example. The point is simply that real common preferences are found when no one is insisting that there can be only one possible outcome.

Necessary knowledge

It is not only issues of behaviour that are targets for coercion and boundary setting. Education is a crucial parenting issue for conventional and TCS parents alike. The supposed need to 'know' certain things or the drive to learn certain things solely in order to keep options open for the future are cornerstones of conventional educational and parenting theory, but are inimical to taking children seriously. In *Doing It Their Way*, I discuss more fully the misconception that there might exist some homogenous body of knowledge that all children should learn by a particular age or even in a particular order. One parent aptly pointed out that when it comes to basic skills, autonomous children will always learn what they need. (*Doing It Their Way* p.47)

We cannot predict the future for our children. By helping them to live their lives now and learn what they want to know now, we can ensure that the knowledge they have is optimum for the particular individual. We help our children to know that new knowledge can always be gained. The push to instil a body of necessary knowledge into our children arises largely from misunderstanding and fear. If we do not make our children learn to read or recite their multiplication tables, will we be doing them a terrible disservice by setting them up for only dead end jobs and a life without choices? If we do not force our children to listen to music or read the plays of Shakespeare, will they forever miss out on rich cultural and aesthetic experiences? If we do not impose some boundaries on our children's learning, will they simply learn nothing?

Children who are coerced by neglect risk enforced ignorance and the closing down of their abilities and passion. This is not the case for children whose autonomy is being respected within homes where parents are providing resources, stimulation, suggestions and support in response to the intrinsic learning motivation of their children. Children will learn to read, multiply, or take photographs, when they have an intrinsic need to acquire that particular skill. Children who are adept at creative problem solving and in finding ways to fulfil their preferences in the present are not likely to stop doing so simply because they reach the age of sixteen or eighteen. Children with choices will become adults with choices. If we do not impose boundaries on our children's learning, but instead help them to learn what they want to learn, how could they possibly learn 'nothing'?

Wasting time

Alongside the mythology of an essential body of knowledge that must be taught at all costs, there is often the idea that learning can be taking place only when certain so-called educational activities are taking place. Other activities - often activities which children particularly enjoy - are conventionally deemed to be of less value or even harmful. Playing computer games, watching so called 'non-educational' TV shows and videos or climbing trees are all things that can be denigrated as wasting time. The TCS philosophy offers a radically different perspective on such 'time wasting'. Time is wasted when it is being spent on things that are extrinsically motivated, that is, when children are doing things they have to do rather than things they want to do. It is possible that our children will make some bad choices, which, by their own lights, turn out to be mistakes. Mistakes can be learnt from, especially when they are our own mistakes and not someone else's imposed agenda. It seems even more likely that a childhood spent learning Shakespeare and physics at someone else's insistence will lead to a life of chronic self-sacrifice and constantly living for tomorrow, while today is miserable. It certainly seems feasible that a childhood spent creatively solving the problem of how to get the most out of life right now will be far from wasted, whatever the particular activities happen to be.

The value of suffering

Conventional parents sometimes object that removing boundaries simply gives children a false notion of what the world is like. They insist that we need to experience a certain level of frustration, hardship and suffering, in order to survive in the real world. It must always be remembered that we all live in the real world. Our circumstances may differ dramatically, but there is still only one world in which we can live. Living well in it is not 'unreal'. Parents who want to impose some frustration or suffering on their child's experience are generally motivated to do so not out of cruelty, but out of fear that otherwise their children will not be prepared for whatever life holds.

The argument for deliberately frustrating our children or sometimes purposefully setting out to 'show' them that they cannot always 'have their own way' is very similar to the argument for natural consequences and is similarly flawed. When parents frustrate their children they are choosing to do so. The hurt is not inevitable, but imposed and artificial. Life contains enough risks and enough learning opportunities for children to see for themselves that bad things happen. They can learn how to tackle and handle the real tragedies and complex problems by having lots of access to information and good models of how to problem-solve creatively. We do not prepare for a journey to a famine-stricken country by starving ourselves, but by building up our strength and learning all we can about basic nutrition and survival. There is no intrinsic value in being in a state of distress. It serves only to crush our ability to think rationally.

Conclusions

We live in a society where children are routinely deprived of the common rights of humanity, where they often cannot choose what to eat or wear, whom they associate with, when they can sleep, what they can learn or even what they can enjoy as leisure. Love is neither compensation nor justification for such a total lack of autonomy. The suffering that arises is not character building or a preparation for living in the real world, but rather, damages the ability to problem solve creatively and consider solutions rationally. It perpetuates an acceptance of suffering and an inability to follow one's preferences into adulthood. Children whose autonomy is respected do not expect to never have to solve problems or that life will be handed to them on a plate or that they will never have to work hard at realising their preferences. Autonomous children know that problem solving is a feature of real life and growth, that risk is inevitable and that change and criticism and new solutions are always going to be needed. What they do not do is conflate problems with suffering or effort with sacrifice. When we live in an ethos of consent, creativity and rationality, boundaries become simply irrelevant.

Chapter seven

Your worst nightmare

Life without boundaries might seem conceivable in certain areas, but most of us have deeply ingrained reservations and entrenched theories about wholesale autonomy. A range of adult fears commonly arises when we consider removing coercion from our children's lives. There is a common fear that if given such autonomy children will become anti-social, a fear that disregards the role of coercion in contributing to anti-social, self-destructive and self-defeating behaviours. In this chapter, I will assert that it is a myth that consent-based parenting is a recipe for producing selfish, uncaring monsters. In doing so, I will briefly consider some of the more 'extreme' scenarios that people imagine might be the result.

Coercion and the anti-social child

Fear and control are common partners. Many parents are afraid that if they are not the ones controlling the child's behaviour, then that behaviour will be 'out of control' rather than within the child's control. Much of this fear arises from watching scenarios where parental control has disintegrated or where parents are so disengaged from their children that the children make increasingly bizarre bids to be noticed and taken seriously. Parents might point to children who are both anti-social and self-destructive and say, 'Look, his parent didn't manage to control him, so we will have to try harder if we don't want our children to end up like that'. Others argue, 'Look, her parents took no interest and simply let her do anything she liked, no questions asked, and what a mess that's resulted in'. These are not arguments against taking children seriously, giving children autonomy or living consensually within our families.

The prisons are not full of TCS children. Whilst TCS is not primarily concerned with outcome- based parenting, I think we can confidently predict that, unless TCS children are living under unjust and illiberal laws, this situation is likely to continue. Self-destructive people who seem to be as much beyond their **own** powers of control as anyone else's are not rational, creative, undamaged individuals. They are those contorted by coercion damage, not those happily pursuing their own best interests.

Why should a child who believes that her parents are on her side, who knows that following her own interests will be supported and facilitated and who believes that solutions can always be found, need to become a sociopath? Many children who become as severely self-destructive as they are anti-social, grow up in homes that veer wildly between strict parenting and neglectful parenting, homes where they can be beaten one moment, ignored the next and screamed at the next. The argument that what we need is more control is false. We cannot possibly be there controlling everything our child does from birth to sixteen-years-old. We physically cannot live their lives. Our children are going to be making decisions and they are going to be making some of those decisions when we are not immediately available. Having built up a repertoire of conversations about every aspect of morality, having spent considerable time sharing criticisms with our children and helping them remain and become creative, rational problem solvers, we can expect that our children will make the best decisions by their own lights at that particular time. We can expect that some mistakes will be made, but making mistakes is an opportunity for learning, not a signal that our autonomy ought to be taken away from us. We can also expect that sometimes our children will not make the decisions that we would have made or advised. Taking children seriously is not an exercise in getting our children to do exactly what we would want by roundabout, manipulative means, even in our absence. Our children will be making new knowledge and pursuing their own interests.   This will not always look like our prescriptions of best interests.

Even in the most rigidly controlling families, where punishment is an ever-present threat and behaviour is controlled by fear, control is ultimately an illusion. Being afraid is as much a motivation for ever more creative acts of deviousness as it is for doing what parents desire; meanwhile, the ability to think rationally about areas pressurised by such chronic coercion becomes an increasingly remote possibility.

The argument that children who are left to their own devices often come up with bad morality or behave in self-destructive ways indicates that children need less autonomy and more firm guidance, is equally flawed. Parents who are serious about living in consent-based relationships with their children do not neglect them. They constantly offer their theories of morality, criticism and information; they facilitate access to conflicting information and counter-arguments; and they constantly engage in conjecture and refutation with their children. What they do not do is cross the line of superseding their children's autonomy or act as if they are infallible. Children who are taken seriously are neither left to their own devices nor coerced.

The selfish monster

Even if we accept that the extremities of anti-social behaviour arise from hideous coercion either through abuse or neglect, we might still have reservations. So our children may not be likely to turn into bank robbers and mass murderers, but will they be pleasant people? Are they not more likely to be spoilt brats who grow up into selfish, petulant adults?

Such questions arise from a number of misunderstandings of self-interest. Firstly, why do we need to oppose self-interest and altruism? We are sadly used to the idea that, if we are enjoying something it must be at someone else's expense, whereas if we are suffering we are helping someone else. Is this really the case? As a parent, I can derive huge satisfaction and pleasure from helping my child get what he wants. It is something I prefer to do. I am at once pursuing my own and my child's interest. As a worker, I can derive enormous satisfaction from my job, or I can choose to do it to support the people I love or to benefit the community. These goals do not need to be mutually exclusive. I am doing what I prefer on one or many levels and others benefit. Similarly, a scientist can pursue her/his passion and make discoveries that are of enormous benefit to humanity, or a researcher can follow her/his passion and create new knowledge of enormous consequence to many lives. It is when we are following our intrinsic motivation that we are both at our most self-interested and most creative, and likely to benefit others in a multiplicity of ways.

Secondly, these questions wrongly assume that we can get inside the minds of others, particularly our children, and label their motivations. Why should a child who wants what he wants be called a 'brat'? What is it that makes us resent his clarity and self-knowledge and sense of self-worth? Are we threatened by attributes that we were not allowed to develop for ourselves as children? Are we afraid that it will mean that our own needs must be subverted? Do we worry that we will have immediately to jump to order and sacrifice our own autonomy? If we have allowed ourselves to enter a cycle of self-sacrifice, then we are not really taking our children any more seriously than we are taking ourselves seriously, and need to address that problem rather than blame our children for it. Having children who can clearly state their initial preferences is a bonus in the process of finding common preferences, not a threat to our own autonomy.

When children experience for themselves relationships of consent in which the needs of others can be taken seriously without infringing their own needs and wants, then they have no reason to fear the needs of others. When children experience the benefits of finding common preferences, then the needs and wants of others become part of the pool of creativity available to them, rather than threats to preferred solutions. A child who will not listen to anything other than his first preference and who irrationally clings to this even when there may be solutions he could enjoy much more, is a child who is used to losing and is determined to resist losing again. Being 'self-centred' or 'pleasing ourselves' does not have to stand in opposition to finding common preferences and benefiting others with our creativity. This is a false and pernicious dichotomy that taking our children seriously can overcome.

Losing control

Adults who have the capacity to determine their own lives and who have the rationality and creativity to live as autonomous people with enlightened self-interest do not routinely act in immoral, self destructive or abusive ways. Yet, we often assume that given the same rights, respect and autonomy, children will do just that. Why? Children may make decisions that we think are bad for them or even wrong in general. Even if we are right, however, it is highly likely that these decisions will arise from the irrationality that accompanies coercion damage. We are not going to convince our children to become more rational and more creative and less self-destructive by coercing them some more. We do not get from a bad situation to a better one by increasing the condition that originally led to the bad situation. It should also be remembered that we might be wrong. It might well be that our child, even a previously coerced child, is in fact not making a bad or immoral decision. They might be making the best and most rational decision possible and one that we, with our own coercion damage and entrenched theories, cannot appreciate. Rational persuasion, conjecture and refutation, creative problem solving, sharing of theories without deciding the outcome for someone else, are all we can offer. The more we offer these, the more effective they become.

Conclusions

However we choose to live our lives, there is but one world currently on offer in which to live it. We all live in the real world, TCS parents and children no less than their conventional counterparts. TCS is an educational theory. It is about problem solving and the growth of knowledge and, as such, is very well placed to enable children to go on to a lifetime of creative problem solving. Living a life of rational self-interest does not mean living a life that is incompatible with negotiating every day problems and situations, but rather gives the flexible and creative tools for doing just that. Being able to follow the rules is only a pragmatic solution when all the variables are in place to make the rules apply. TCS goes significantly beyond this. It frees people to do the kind of creative and rational thinking that is not merely optimum for negotiating the world in a pragmatic sense, but which also maximises genuine learning and ensures a moral approach to decisions. It recognises that in the real world, as much as in the theoretical world, acting out of self-interest is not monstrous or dangerous, but is a way of maximising best interest and creativity in general. When people follow their intrinsic motivation and self-interest, they maximise the very creativity which is vital to new ideas and progress for everyone. Individual happiness is a building block of progress, not an obstacle to it. The real world benefits most from creative, rational, self-interested, intrinsically motivated problem solvers.

This does not mean that such children will be uninterested in criticism and the best theories of others, especially of parents whom they can trust not to coerce them. Genuinely rational and creative self-interested people are constantly in pursuit of better knowledge, better theories, and better solutions. They are not threatened by input, even when it contradicts a current piece of understanding. Why should a child who knows that she is not going to be coerced feel threatened by a piece of information or an opinion that contradicts something she had previously thought? Such a child can afford to listen to diverse opinions, to take her time evaluating arguments, to take risks. Such a child can afford to trust that her parent is offering genuine advice and is as open-minded as she is.

Of course, our children will make mistakes. We are each fallible; but mistakes, as much as solutions, can provide points of growth. No system of parenting can predict the future for our children or guarantee them a life without problems. Such a life would, in any case, be sterile and empty of any growth of knowledge. By fostering their autonomy and building models of consent, flexibility, creativity and rationality, TCS gives children the freedom to find their own solutions in the real world and gives the world the prospect of highly creative thinkers from whom to benefit.

Chapter eight

Education for all, a life for all

In this final chapter, I will look briefly at the link between non-coercive lifestyles and autonomous learning. I will go on to propose that the philosophy outlined in the preceding chapters is one that not only fosters the growth of knowledge across a whole range of learning environments, but also enables vastly divergent families and individuals to find structures of consent. Finally, I will sum up some of the key differences between conventional and consent-based parenting, concluding that consent-based parenting and education is the only style that does not damage autonomy and which allows for a consistently positive framework for negotiating family living and learning.

An environment for learning

Taking Children Seriously is not so much a parenting theory as a moral theory for family interaction and an educational theory about how knowledge grows. If we assume that coercion damages thinking, then a non-coercive environment must be the best learning environment possible. We do not think rationally about areas that we associate with distress. Distress lessens our grasp of rationality and creativity and so hampers our learning. That does not mean that all coerced people will grow up stupid and ignorant, but it does mean that in areas in which people experience coercion, they are later likely to encounter greater numbers of thinking difficulties. It also means that areas of creativity are being nipped in the bud. So we might end up with, for example, a maths genius who cannot form intimate relationships and has very poor practical money handling skills; an artist who finds every journey horrifically stressful and cannot think rationally about doing laundry, and so on.

This is not to say that TCS is an outcome based parenting philosophy. The idea is not to produce the 'best' product, but to facilitate the child to live the best life by her own lights, which will not happen if we introduce thinking problems along the way through systematic coercion. Eradicating coercion then becomes fundamental to real education. True education is about gaining knowledge in those areas in which one wants to gain knowledge.

It is quite possible to force our children to learn certain things in a behaviourist, outcome-based fashion. TCS, however, proposes that this is both morally wrong and will result in thinking damage in one or more areas. The key is intrinsic motivation, learning the things we want to learn. Who better to know what learning is most needed, wanted and appropriate, than the person himself? What other form of learning could be more efficient? Learning is something that takes place in an individual's mind - it cannot be poured in as though people were empty buckets waiting to be filled. Knowledge grows when it is intrinsic to the learner, and it is only taking children seriously that can give the degree of autonomy needed for this process to flourish.

Living consensually with our children impacts on every area of life. We cannot respect our children's autonomy if we are choosing what they should and should not learn. Although, in many, if not most cases, this will mean that children will choose home-based education as the optimum context for their autonomous learning, some children will choose school environments. In Chapter Two above, I considered how children can use what would seem to be highly coercive environments. When children are free to choose whether or not to be in school, they are free to take what they need or want from the experience. Their freedom transforms the nature of their relationship with the institution, and they know that their parents will assist them in dealing with the institution. There may be good and rational reasons why a particular child might choose, at some time, to use various kinds of structured learning, including schools. Sometimes, what the child is looking for can be found in other, better environments; but autonomy in education, as in life, is not about the style of learning, but about who has the control and motivation.

An inclusive paradigm

Taking Children Seriously is an educational philosophy that covers the whole gamut of learning environments. Nevertheless, it should be noted that many autonomously educated children find that schools are not the best environments for learning and that, on balance, home-based education is more likely to provide them with the optimum conditions for intrinsically motivated growth of knowledge. Living consensually with our children is a moral principle to be applied to all parent-child relationships. It is not just another parenting theory that might be applicable to only some children. TCS is not just for parents of especially bright children, or especially compliant children, or especially reasonable children. I have heard the objection that TCS is all very well if it 'works', or that it is fine if you have the 'right' sort of children on whom it will work. This objection totally misses the point of making the paradigm shift needed to live consensually within families. The question is not whether the theory 'works', but whether it is ever 'right' to coerce another autonomous human being, by virtue of their age or any other criteria.

Let us think of another area of morality to sharpen the question: is it right for husbands to beat their wives? Most people in this society at this time would say 'No!' Some might talk about understanding special conditions, but barring the most extreme of mitigating circumstances, we could probably reach a consensus that this type of coercion between a husband and wife is wrong. Getting back to parents and children, the first question that parents contemplating TCS need to ask themselves is: Is coercion a proper way to treat my children? If the answer is no, then questions of whether it is practical or not become issues of finding ways to do the right thing, rather than ways of justifying why we have to do the wrong thing.

It is not moral to rob another human of his or her autonomy in order to produce the specimen that parents most desire. Many theories of parenting are primarily concerned with how little Sam is going to 'turn out'. There is a strong cultural pull towards proving that Sam is going to 'do well' or 'do us proud'. This is perhaps especially true when we are already going against the flow by home educating and feel that we are under scrutiny to show that our way is just as good, if not better, by producing results. TCS assumes that every individual of any age is an autonomous agent. TCS assumes that it is wrong to coerce your own child. If this is the case, then trying to work towards specific outcomes in parenting, whether to seek cultural approval or for our own inner glow, is not supportable. Many of the parenting philosophies that do advocate outcomes do so in very reasonable language, and look as though they have very laudable goals, which any right-thinking person would support. What could be wrong with wanting your child to be happy, flexible, goal-oriented, and morally upright? The problem is simply that all such terms tend to be loaded with agenda and sliding meanings. TCS promotes the child's own autonomy by his or her own lights. The likelihood is that this will have good effects in the child's life, but the child must be in control of defining those effects. We must share our own morality with the child, but the child must ultimately be free to decide how to act. There is no testable end-product. We are talking about autonomous human beings brought up in fallible human households, not control specimens who can become advertisements for how well we parented.

Taking Children Seriously proposes no blue print solutions to problems. It is essentially a process rather than a set of guidelines, and a moral way of relating rather than just another outcome-based parenting theory. It is this that enables the theory to encompass anyone and everyone.

Living without boundaries

Childcare 'experts' sometimes propose that giving our children 'firm boundaries' is a way of giving them the security they need and crave. It is true that such boundaries can give a sense of safety, but they often do so at a high cost. Along with the protection comes a hunger for a lifetime of security and certainty, an unwillingness to ask too many uncomfortable questions, and a dangerous willingness to obey without question. Fostering intrinsic security, however, is a much more complex process. To be able to find solutions; to enter into a process of conjecture and refutation; to listen to and weigh criticism and advice before making decisions; to take responsibility for one's decisions: this is another kind of security, which is eminently more valuable.

Boundaries are artificial, the made-up rules to which autonomous human beings are always the exception. *Taking Children Seriously* proposes a process of finding common preferences by which each problem can find its unique solution. Working with this process demands a whole new paradigm. It is with this paradigm switch in mind that I present a summary of some of the key differences between conventional and consent-based parenting.

CONVENTIONAL PARENTING	CONSENT-BASED PARENTING
The parent is authoritative. This may be a strict authority, or a liberal regime, in which the parent is the 'ultimate' or 'bottom line' arbitrator.	The parent acknowledges fallibility. The parent offers trusted advice, theories and criticism.

The conventional parent may listen, negotiate or compromise before making the final decision.	The parent takes the child seriously to reach a common preference and respects the child's autonomy.
The parent operates from some standard of what is in the child's 'best interest' or 'own good'.	The parent operates from the principle that autonomous humans of all ages are the ultimate best judge of their own best interest and assumes that coercion damages the ability to think rationally.
Parents may offer loving guidance within a framework of boundaries.	Parents believe that love is not a good reason to compromise another's autonomy. Love does not justify abandoning morality.
Various frameworks are used to supply the boundaries. These may be so-called 'natural' consequences, 'common sense', inherited memes, religious or ideological frameworks or (most often), a combination of the above.	There are no artificial boundaries. The participants use rationality and creativity to reach common preferences and create new knowledge to solve problems.
Parents regularly have outcomes in mind, both in terms of short term desired behaviour or long term general attributes.	Parents do not attempt to either prescribe or predict outcomes.
Parents decide ahead of solutions being sought that some problems are intractable and not capable of 'win-win' outcomes, so they must sometimes impose a solution in which only some win or a compromise in which no-one wins.	Parents believe that there are always solutions. They hold that sometimes we fail to find solutions because of our limited creativity and rationality and because we are fallible, but they assume that solutions (in which all win), are, at least theoretically, always possible.
Parents may posit a 'contract' between themselves and their children in which they provide food, warmth, shelter, protection and acceptance whilst their	Parents acknowledge an asymmetrical relationship between themselves and their children, in which their parental responsibility is not matched by a corresponding duty or obligation on the part of

children owe various levels of duty or obedience.	children who were never free to decide to enter (or not), into such a contract.
Coercion is sometimes used as being preferable to some other bad, which is perceived as worse (e.g. forced tooth brushing is better than possible tooth decay).	Parents do not believe that it is right to act immorally in order to obtain a good outcome.
Parents often believe that they are better placed to make decisions for their children on the basis of superior experience.	Parents non-coercively offer their experience, but do not assume that they are right. Whilst experience can be useful, it can also be fallible and subject to previous coercion damage, so all participants should subject all input to a process of conjecture and refutation. Lack of experience should not be used to dehumanise children or to make them appear less that full autonomous moral agents.
Children who get what they want become spoiled and selfish. Parents are in position best to know the limits of their resources and to make it clear that children cannot 'have everything'.	A spoilt child is a child in distress who can never be satisfied. Parents assume that children can be both 'self-centred' and act morally and that these things are not mutually exclusive. Parents realise that getting what we want is not equivalent to having everything. The aim is not immediately to meet every demand, but to find creative common preference solutions.
Parents may impose boundaries out of a fear of self-sacrifice or being coerced by their children.	Parents recognise that the balance of power rests with them and that they need to redress this imbalance. The aim is always to achieve mutual consent and find common preference solutions. Self-sacrifice may sometimes be a failure default, but is not to be tolerated as a chronic or regular outcome.

Parents assume that there are certain things that children just have to be taught. It is irresponsible of parents not to ensure that these 'basics' are learned, even if this sometimes means resorting to coercion.	Parents recognise that if there were such a list of 'essential things children must learn' then coercive parenting theories would be able to agree on what this list must contain, but there is no such agreement. Parents assume that if certain things are important or essential for children to survive in modern society, then there is no reason why a rational, creative, autonomous child would not learn them without coercion.
Parents assume that childhood is a preparation for life in the real or adult world and it is the parents' responsibility to equip children for this.	Parents assume that children's present life is intrinsically valuable of itself and that finding solutions to today's problems is not only the best way to live now, but will also tend to assist children to remain creative, flexible problem solvers.

In conclusion, *Taking Children Seriously* is the only philosophy that does not damage autonomy and which allows for a consistently positive framework for negotiating family living and learning. It is a moral and educational paradigm, which furnishes families not with a list of guidelines, but with a process for solving problems in which everyone wins.

> *"... I don't know the future. I didn't come here to tell you how this is going to end. I came here to tell you how it's going to begin ... I'm going to show them ... a world without rules or controls, without borders or boundaries, a world where anything is possible. Where we go from there is a choice I leave to you."*
>
> (*The Matrix*, closing scene)

References and further reading

Clarke, Arthur C (July 1973) *2001, A Space Odyssey,* London:Arrow Books
Dobson, James (1993) *Dare to Discipline*, Vida Publishing
Fortune-Wood, Jan (2000) *Doing it Their Way,* Nottingham:Educational Heretics Press
Haak, Carl *from* www.rsglh.org.parental.discipline.html
Lawrence, Sarah *articles in TCS Journal & website www.tcs.ac*
Liedlof, Jean (1989) *The Continuum Concept*, Arkana
Popper, Karl (1995) *The Myth of the Framework,* London:Routledge
Popper, Karl (1995) *In Search of a Better World*, London:Routledge

Websites to which reference is made.

www.attachmentparenting.org
www.gn.apc.org/edheretics
www.home-education.org.ukwww.parenting.org
www.positiveparenting.com
www.tcs.ac

Films referred to:

Liar, Liar (1997) Universal City Studios
The Matrix (1999) Warner Brothers, Village Roadshow Films (BV) Ltd